Flower
Arranging

JOHN WILEY & SONS CANADA LIMITED

First published in Canada 1980
by John Wiley & Sons, Canada Limited

Designed and produced by
Grisewood and Dempsey Limited
141–143 Drury Lane London WC2
© Grisewood and Dempsey Limited
1980

Printed and bound by
Vallardi Industrie Grafiche S.p.A. Milan

Author
Daphne Vagg

Illustrator
Wendy Lewis

Editors
Christopher Tunney
Diane James

Consultant
Jean Taylor

Canadian Cataloguing in Publication Data
Vagg, Daphne.
  Flower arranging

  (A Kingfisher leisure guide)

ISBN 0-471-99869-9

1. Flower arrangement. I. Title. II. Series.

SB449.V35   745.92   C80-094062-8

Contents

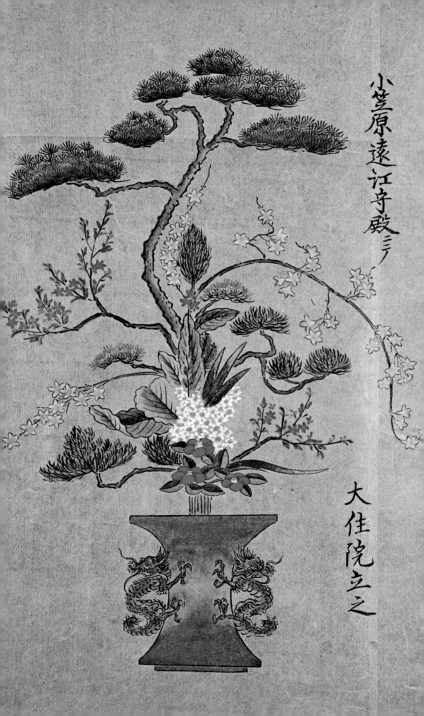

Introduction

Many people mistakenly think of flower arranging as a hobby and an interest only for those who have big gardens or who can afford to buy large quantities of flowers. Having a garden is certainly a help, but the would-be flower arranger's greatest asset is an enthusiasm for natural materials: flowers and leaves are only two of the many types of material used in arrangements today. Indeed, some arrangements use no flowers at all.

Suitable materials can be easily collected during trips into the country (tree branches, bark, cones, twigs, moss) or to the seaside (shells, seaweed curls, interesting pieces of flotsam and jetsam). Pot plants can be used time and time again in different arrangements. And at each season of the year, some flowers or other plant materials are relatively cheap.

Flower arrangement is an art form that can satisfy the creative need we all have. And the medium it uses is one that is already beautiful or interesting in itself. The arranger chooses from a limitless bounty and tries to create new beauty.

Left: An early Chinese painting of a formal flower arrangement.

Below: A traditional massed arrangement in an informal style.

The Flower Arranger's Materials

Flower arranging, unlike many other crafts, requires very little initial equipment. To begin with, ordinary household items such as a pair of kitchen scissors or a sharp knife, a jug, vase, or bowl are sufficient to achieve a satisfactory result. Add to these items a bunch of flowers—tulips, dahlias, roses, daffodils, or a mixed bunch from the garden—and an arrangement is at once possible.

It is not necessary to be particularly artistic to make a pleasing flower arrangement, but there are a few snags and problems involved in flower arranging that require a certain amount of 'inside information'.

Home-made Stem Supports or 'Mechanics'

Providing a large vase or jug is used for an arrangement of flowers of similar size, there will be no problem as the flowers will support each other and not droop or flop over the side of the vase. However, if an arrangement is to be made in a shallow container, or particularly long stems are to be used, some form of support or anchor is necessary to keep the flowers in place.

This support is an essential piece of the flower arranger's equipment. But if a proper support is not available there are several ways of creating a substitute using simple household items. However, these are temporary measures, and not as efficient as the real thing.

Home-Made Stem Supports

Right: A jam jar or narrow-necked vase placed in the middle of a shallow bowl will support tall stems that would otherwise flop over. The arrangement should be made in such a way that the jar or vase does not show.

Below: An effective support can be made by stuffing crumpled newspaper firmly into a jug or jar, and making it into a pulp with water. Flower stems can then be pushed into the pulp, and will be held securely in place. An equally good support can be made by crisscrossing strips of Sellotape over the open end of a vase or jar. Flower stems are pushed into the holes between the strips.

Crumpled newspaper

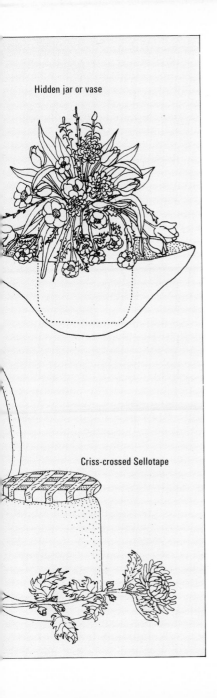

Hidden jar or vase

Criss-crossed Sellotape

When short-stemmed material is to be arranged in a tall vase, the vase should be filled three-quarters full with sand. Water is added, and the flowers arranged in the sand. The container must not be too large for the size of plant material to be used.

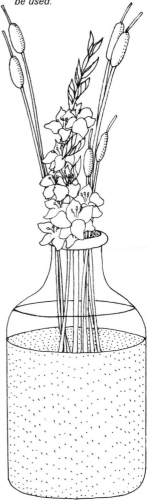

Mechanics to Buy

Stem supports for flower arrangements are manufactured in a variety of shapes, sizes, and materials. Most flower arrangers keep a selection of shapes and sizes to fit their favourite containers. Supports are referred to as *mechanics*. They can be bought in a florist's shop, garden centre, or hardware shop, or from a stall at a flower show.

Pinholders

Pinholders are sometimes called *needlepoint holders* or *kenzans*. They are relatively expensive, but are essential pieces of equipment. With care they should last a lifetime. The ideal pinholder should have sharp, rustless metal pins, not less than 2 cm long. The pins should be set closely together and cover the whole area of the heavy lead base. The stems are spiked onto or between the pins, and the weight of the lead base keeps the arrangement in place. Plastic pinholders should be avoided, and, similarly, pinholders with rubber suction as they tend to work themselves loose in water. The very small sizes of pinholder have a limited use, and the most useful size to start with is a round shape 60 to 80 mm in diameter. Rectangular and crescent shapes are also available.

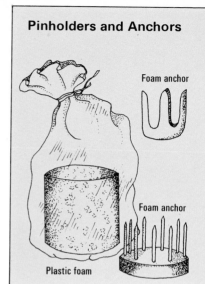

Pinholders and Anchors

Foam anchor

Foam anchor

Plastic foam

Wire Mesh

Wire mesh is also known as *chicken wire* or *wire netting*. Crumpled wire mesh is one of the most popular supports used by flower arrangers. Used in conjunction with a pinholder it will support almost any arrangement. The mesh can be bought from an ironmonger, and 1 metre of 50 mm wire mesh will provide enough for use in three or four average size containers. Smaller mesh is useful for covering blocks of water-retaining foam. If possible plastic-coated mesh should not be used as it is more

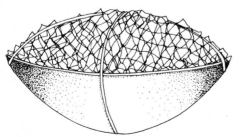

Crumpled wire mesh makes an effective support for arrangements. It should form a dome above the top of the container. Two rubber bands criss-crossed over the mesh and container make it secure. The bands can be cut away if they show through.

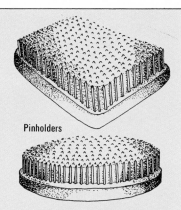

Pinholders

Above: Pinholders have heavy lead bases and rustless pins.

Left: Water-retaining foam can be kept damp by storing it in a polythene bag.

difficult to disguise in an arrangement. A heavy gauge of mesh is difficult to crumple, and hard on the hands. If a silver or delicate porcelain container is to be used it should be lined with aluminium foil or with polythene sheeting before putting the mesh in.

Plastic Foam

Water-retaining plastic foam is available under various brand names, but as the Oasis brand was first, most flower arrangers use this name. There is very little difference between the various brands of foam, and they all provide an efficient means of supporting stems. The foam is usually green and is sold in blocks measuring 22 × 10 × 7 cms, and also in rounds of 8 cm diameter, 5 cm in depth. The foam can be easily cut with a knife to fit any container. It is light and easy to carry when dry, but it is capable of absorbing a large amount

of water which makes it heavy and stable. In most cases it can be used more than once, but it does have a limited life. The brown, granular blocks, similar in size and shape to the green foam blocks do not absorb water and are used for making arrangements with dried, preserved or artificial flowers.

Foam Anchors

Foam anchors are used to hold foam blocks firmly in a container so that they do not slip or fall over when the arrangement is complete. A metal anchor has a heavy base, similar to that of a pinholder, but has fewer, longer pins. The most efficient anchors have eight pins about 5 cm long in a lead base with a diameter of 5 cm. A smaller, less expensive plastic anchor about 3 cm in diameter, with 4 prongs about 3 cm long, is also available. This small holder is excellent for small arrangements not more than about 25 cm high.

Fixatives

Fixatives are needed to secure pinholders and foam anchors to the container. There are a number of floral clays on the market, or Plasticine can be used as an alternative. They can be easily removed afterwards from the container with a swab dipped in turpentine or white spirit.

Security Measures

Green sticky tape, reel wire, rubber bands, or string can be used to make certain that all mechanics will stay in place. There is nothing more frustrating than spending time on an arrangement that falls over the minute it is finished.

Other Equipment

A few more pieces of simple equipment completes the flower arranger's 'tools of the trade'.

Cutters

Flower scissors have short blades, often with serrated edges and a special notch for cutting thin wire. Garden secateurs are useful for cutting thick branches and woody stems. A penknife, craft knife, or old sharp kitchen knife can be used for various jobs—cutting Oasis, scraping stems, or removing floral clay from the bottom of pinholders or containers.

Buckets

Buckets are needed to stand flowers and leaves in before and while making the arrangement. An ordinary household bucket will do, but one with special side handles is even better. Having handles at the side means that there is less danger of crushing the flower heads.

Below: One or two buckets are needed for soaking the stems of cut flowers and leaves. Special buckets with side handles are ideal, as there is less risk of crushing the flower heads; but, to begin with, ordinary household buckets are adequate. The buckets should be filled to the top with water, and the flowers and branches placed in them for at least two hours before arranging.

*Bottom: Flower scissors have short blades that are usually serrated and that often have a special notch for cutting wire.
A long-spouted, plastic watering-can is useful for topping-up arrangements.*

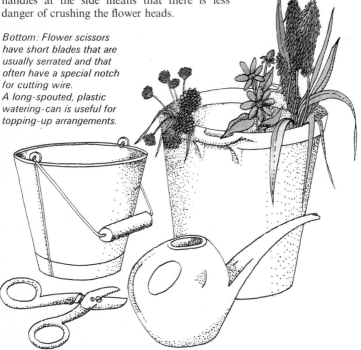

14

Watering Cans

Cans with long spouts are the most useful, particularly those of the type used for watering house-plants. Containers can then be filled up with water without disturbing the flower arrangement.

Sprays

Misting sprays are not essential, but no experienced flower arranger would be without one. It is used to spray arrangements with water to keep a moist atmosphere around them, and so prolong their life.

Wire

Stub wires of various lengths and gauges are useful, as are short rose wires. They can usually be bought in small packets and only a few are needed to start with. Fine reel wire is also useful for securing mechanics.

Tool Box

It is a good idea to get into the habit of keeping flower arranging tools and equipment together in a box. A plastic one with a lid is ideal. Keep several disposable cloths in it for cleaning up any spilt water.

A small misting spray, of the type sold for use in the greenhouse or with houseplants, is suitable for spraying arrangements to preserve a moist atmosphere around them. This reduces transpiration and prolongs the life of the plant material.

Extras

Clamps Driftwood can sometimes be difficult to fix in an arrangement in the position required. Special clamps can be purchased that overcome this problem unobtrusively. Usually, they have a base that makes it possible to attach them securely to a pinholder.

Florist's tape has many uses, including 'first aid'. It is particularly useful for binding stems in dried flower arrangements.

Funnels, either purchased or home-made, can help to solve many problems. Short-stemmed flowers, which could not otherwise be used in a tall arrangement, can be supported in a raised funnel at the desired height. Because the funnel has a closed end, the flowers can be given their own water supply.

Nail scissors, small enough to use for intricate work in grooming, can sometimes be of more help than flower scissors and are usually readily available.

Containers

The word *container* is used to describe anything that can be made to hold water, and can be used for a flower arrangement. Simple containers are usually the most effective. An elaborate vase or bowl, with a complicated shape and colourful decoration, will compete with the arrangement for the viewer's attention. Using an ornate container also makes it more difficult to create a pleasing harmony between the arrangement and the container. Strong patterns and pictorial decorations should be avoided.

Colours

Containers in neutral, muted colours are most useful for general use. Grey, brown, green, and all earthy colours will combine happily with any arrangement. Metallic finishes such as bronze, copper, silver, pewter, and gilt—providing they are not too highly polished—make a good foil for most plant materials. Matt surfaces are generally more effective than shiny ones. The colour of the container is not always important: often the vase is concealed by flowers or foliage.

Shapes

Before mechanics such as pinholders and plastic foam were available, it was usually necessary to have a deep container if the flowers were to be able to stand in water. The invention of water-retaining foams in the middle of this century, meant that it was no longer important to use a deep container, and now a far greater variety of flower arrangement containers are available.

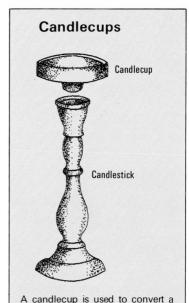

Candlecups

Candlecup

Candlestick

A candlecup is used to convert a candlestick or a narrow-necked vase into a container to hold an arrangement. The candlecup fits into the neck of the candlestick or vase and is large enough to hold a piece of plastic foam.

A plastic urn is a less expensive container than those made from pottery or glass.

Containers for almost every need. Several of them are plastic and cost very little. Others are homemade: the tall silver vase is, in fact, a bleach bottle with its top cut off and then sprayed with silver paint; the black-painted tin once contained baked beans. The white Victorian candlestick was a junk shop find; it is fitted with a candlecup to hold Oasis. Other containers are common household items —a pet's bowl, a soup dish, and a rectangular earthenware dish.

Collecting Containers

A modest collection of containers is neither difficult nor expensive to assemble. It might include the following, some of which may already be available in the home, and the others, inexpensive to buy: a cereal or soup bowl, an old vegetable dish or soup tureen, a modern casserole or pie dish, a wine glass, a candlestick fitted with a *candlecup* made for the purpose of holding a support, a dog bowl, a plastic saucer to hold a round of Oasis, a plastic urn, a low basket with a handle or lid, and a box with a hinged lid—the last two having a tin, plastic box, or carton inside to hold water.

It is never a good idea to buy an expensive container before gaining some experience of arranging. It so often turns out to be a white elephant because the choice was made with insufficient knowledge. The basic list mentioned can be supplemented by home-made containers. Once the collection is started it can be added to as experience suggests useful shapes, sizes, and colours to suit your home and particular style of arranging.

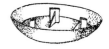

Oasis saucers are designed to hold a standard size cylinder of foam. One variety has a built-in rim that holds the foam firmly in place. Another has thin triangular wedges that the wet foam can be spiked onto.

Making Containers

Apart from the satisfaction of making a good flower arrangement, there is nothing quite so rewarding as making a container to suit your own requirements, especially as it can be done very cheaply.

Take a careful second look before throwing away plastic bottles such as those used for detergent, bleach, soft drinks, cooking oil, and bath salts. Cartons that once contained cream, margarine, yoghurt, and cheese, and different shapes and sizes of tins are all potential containers for flower arrangements. If the shape is good, the colour and texture can soon be changed.

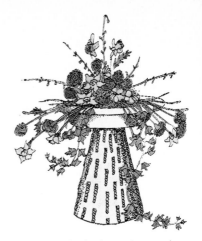

A raised container can be made from an old lampshade or a cardboard cone with the point cut off. A plastic saucer can be fixed on top with Oasisfix or Bostik No. 5. Pasta shapes can be used to decorate the base.

Food tins, plastic cartons, and bottles (with the tops cut off) can all be decorated with string or sea-grass to make effective containers. First, a 2-cm band of glue should be applied to the top of the container. String is then wound round neatly, and the end tucked under the first two or three rows. The last two or three rows should be treated in the same way.

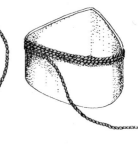

Below: Sand can be applied over a layer of glue to alter the surface texture.

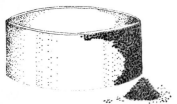

Colouring Containers

Most plastic bottles, cartons, and tins will take a coat of matt emulsion paint provided the surface is 'keyed' first by rubbing with a medium-grade sandpaper.

Blackboard paint is available in matt black or dark green, and both are useful for painting containers. Metallic spray paints have the advantage of giving a less shiny finish

18

than the real thing—silver, gold, copper, bronze, or brass.

Car retouching sprays are available in a vast range of colours. These paints are less dense than others and need an undercoat, particularly if there is lettering to cover up. If shoe polish is brushed or rubbed over a surface it can reduce a shine that is too eye-catching, or tone down a strong colour.

Altering the Texture

Sand or plaster can be mixed with emulsion paint to give a rough tex-

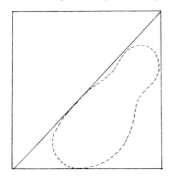

ture. Alternatively, lentils, seeds, pasta shapes, beads, or cut-out cardboard shapes can be glued onto a tin or plastic carton before painting.

A tin or low dish covered with kitchen foil can be given a pewter effect. The foil is glued to the tin. Leave any small wrinkles or lines that occur. Black gloss paint or shoe polish is then brushed over the foil and rubbed off again before it dries. The black will take the shine off the foil and remain in the crevices to give the effect of antique pewter.

A tin or plastic bottle without its lid can be covered with string, twine, or sea-grass. The string, starting from the top, is wound round and round, and the rows glued down securely. Three or four clothes pegs clipped over the first two rows will hold them in place until the glue is dry.

Hessian, rush matting, or fabric can be glued over any container with straight sides. A cake board could be covered with the same material to make a matching base.

Old sheeting, dipped in thick wallpaper paste, can be pressed in random folds onto a container. This will give the effect of rough textured pottery. When quite dry, the container can be sprayed or painted.

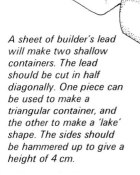

A sheet of builder's lead will make two shallow containers. The lead should be cut in half diagonally. One piece can be used to make a triangular container, and the other to make a 'lake' shape. The sides should be hammered up to give a height of 4 cm.

Accessories and Bases

Household ornaments, souvenirs, or holiday finds can often provide inspiration for a flower arrangement. Such objects are usually termed *accessories*. They may be used within the arrangement itself or as part of a planned grouping with the flowers. This type of mixed group is often used for flower show exhibits or exhibition displays, but of course it can also be very decorative in the home. When using accessories, a number of considerations must be borne in mind.

Dominance
In competitions, an accessory should not normally be the most dominant feature. Elsewhere, of course, the size relationship between accessory and flowers can be whatever the décor or occasion demands. However, the two parts should never be given equal importance, or the arrangement will lose impact.

Style
The flowers and the accessory should relate in style. A Victorian souvenir would not complement a very modern driftwood design, and a stylized torso sculpture would be strangely paired with flowers in a traditional triangular arrangement.

Colour
There should be a colour link between the accessory and the rest of the arrangement. One of the pleasures of making this sort of design is seeking plant material with colours that enhance the arrangement. Often, quite unexpected small colour accents and links are found that delight the eye.

Shape and Line
The whole form of the arrangement and its principal line should extend

Right top and centre: Different bases can be used to set off arrangements. The green table mat is well suited to the stark modern design, and the silver-coloured cakeboard complements the more traditional arrangement.

Right: The pottery Madonna is used as an accessory for this arrangement of hyacinth and daffodils.

Fabric covered cake board

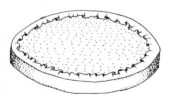

Wood slice

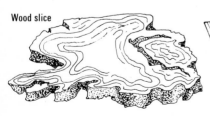

Table mat

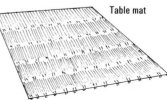

or in some way complement the accessory. Or it may repeat the line of the accessory.

Levels
Generally, it makes for better grouping if the flower arrangement and the accessory are on slightly different levels. Depending on the relative sizes, shapes, and colours, one of them can be raised on a small extra base or concealed block.

Scale
When two or more accessories are used, they need to be in proper proportion to each other. This is especially important in a landscape 'scene' where the illusion can be quite destroyed if a large bird ornament, for example, is near a cat figurine. The size relationship between the accessory and the plant material is important too. A delicate figurine can be made to look ridiculous by the proximity of an over-large flower or leaf.

Several small accessories are often better grouped together rather than dotted round the design. A preliminary arrangement of the plant materials and the accessories often helps in judging balance and proportions. An accessory should never appear to have been added as an afterthought; it must be an integral part of the design.

Bases
It helps to unify the design if flowers and accessory are grouped on one base. This might be a wooden board, a tray, a piece of marble or stone, a place mat, or a board covered with a suitable fabric. But too large a base can dwarf the main features, and should be avoided.

21

Making the Most of Flowers and Leaves

Whenever possible flowers and leaves should be gathered in the early morning when the water content in plants is at its highest Avoid picking in the heat of the day when plants may be lacking water because of rapid transpiration.

It is better to cut stems with secateurs, flower scissors, or a sharp knife than to break them with the fingers, and perhaps tear them. The flower and leaf stems should be put in water as soon as possible. When gathering flowers, a bucket half filled with water is much more practical than a basket. If a bucket is not available make sure that the flowers and leaves are not left lying in the sun.

It is important to choose carefully where and what you cut. The bush or plant should still look attractive and balanced afterwards. Either cut stems at a junction with another stem, at a leaf axil—where a leaf joins the stem—or close to the ground, so that ugly chopped-off stem ends do not spoil the look of the garden.

Decide before picking exactly what flowers and foliage will be necessary for the arrangement; this will cut down on waste afterwards. Also, remember the size of the proposed design. If a large vase or bowl is to be used, some stems will need to be at least one and a half times the height of the vase. Size and length can be very deceptive to the eye, indoors and out. If there is any doubt it is worth measuring the stem.

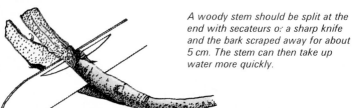

A woody stem should be split at the end with secateurs or a sharp knife and the bark scraped away for about 5 cm. The stem can then take up water more quickly.

Badly damaged, holed, or stained leaves must be removed, and over-crowded leaves thinned out. But it is important to consider the effect on the balance and decorative value of the spray.

Preparing Stems

Preliminary cutting and trimming will ensure that cut plant material lasts longer, and will also make the material easier to arrange. Firstly, remove any damaged, faded, or overcrowded flowers and leaves, and then remove all leaves from the lower part of the stem. If these lower leaves are left on, they will almost certainly be under water, and will soon make the water smell very unpleasant.

Any snags and thorns should be cut off, and the end of the stem trimmed about 10 mm from the end using a slanting cut. On woody stems and branches, the bark should be scraped away for about 50 mm at the end. This helps the uptake of water.

The old practice of hammering stem ends is not recommended because it crushes the ends so much that the stems will not stand on a pinholder and may be difficult to push into foam. It is always possible to recut above the crushed part, but doing so has the dis-advantage that valuable stem length may be lost. Each stem should be put back into the bucket of water as soon as it has been dealt with.

All leaves likely to be below the water-line in the finished arrangement should be removed. At least 5 or 6 cm at the end of the stem should be completely clear.

Side shoots may have to be removed to improve the line. Thorns should be broken off for ease of handling, and to avoid making unnecessarily large holes in plastic foam.

A colourful flower market by La Madeleine in Paris. All the flowers are standing in buckets of water and are shaded as far as possible by awnings.
Once flowers have been cut, they need protection from hot sun, cold winds, and draughts. If they are subjected to any of these extremes, they will dry out too quickly and will not last well in an arrangement.
Flowers bought from a barrow or street stall are often cheaper than those sold in a shop. But the buyer should look carefully for signs indicating a lack of freshness.

Buying

The best advice when buying cut flowers is to go to a reliable florist, grower, market, or nurseryman. But even when buying from a reputable source, there are several things to bear in mind when choosing cut flowers.

Most flowers are best bought when in bud but with a little petal colour showing. The 'vase-life' of fully open flowers is bound to be shorter than that of those in bud, and many people enjoy watching buds opening out in the vase. Sometimes, on a market or street stall, open flowers are cheaper as they have been reduced for a quick

sale. If they are only required to last for a short while, such as for a party, they may well be a good buy.

All spring flowers, especially daffodils, narcissi, anemones, and tulips, should have some petal colour showing so that the colour of the flowers can be determined. And, if there is no colour showing it means they may have been cut so tightly budded that they will never open.

Flowers growing in a spike, or along a branch, such as gladioli, delphiniums, larkspurs, or freesias, should have buds still waiting to blossom. Only the lower florets should be fully out. Daisy-type flower centres should have a greenish appearance and still be tight.

Long-stemmed flowers are usually more expensive than shorter ones of the same type, so avoid paying extra for long stems if they are not needed. If stems are floppy, brown, or slimy when they are taken out of the water in the shop or market, it means that they have been there for a long time and should not be bought.

Flowers should be standing in water, and not still lying in their packing boxes where their stems will be drying out. Sometimes growers cut flowers directly from the plant so

that this problem does not arise. If the flowers have been standing for a long time in full sunlight, by a radiator, on a draughty street corner, or where passers-by have constantly brushed past them, the vase-life will already have been seriously shortened.

Flowers bought from a stall or market should be fully wrapped, not just the stems, as it is the flower heads that need the most protection. The flowers should be taken home as soon as possible, and not left lying in a car in hot sun. Once the stems have been prepared they should be placed at once in deep water in a cool place.

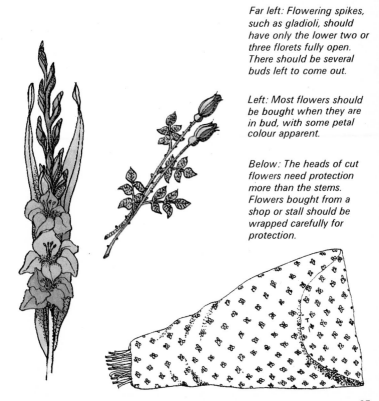

Far left: Flowering spikes, such as gladioli, should have only the lower two or three florets fully open. There should be several buds left to come out.

Left: Most flowers should be bought when they are in bud, with some petal colour apparent.

Below: The heads of cut flowers need protection more than the stems. Flowers bought from a shop or stall should be wrapped carefully for protection.

25

Conditioning

Conditioning means any treatment that can be administered to prolong the life of cut plant material. This usually means restoring the plant's water supply as quickly and effectively as possible, Some plants, however, need more specialized treatment than others.

Soaking the Stems
The most important basic treatment is to soak the stems in a bucket of deep water—preferably warm—for several hours before arranging them. It is even better if they can be left in the bucket over-night. The bucket should be left in the coolest place possible.

Burning the Stem Ends
Poppies, spurges, and poinsettias exude a milky liquid when they are cut. To stop the loss of liquid their stem ends need to be singed in a flame in order to seal them. A lighted match can be used, but a candle or a gas burner is better. The stem ends are held in the flame until they are blackened. They should then be left to stand in deep water.

Boiling the Stem Ends
Although this treatment sounds drastic, it is often very effective. Very young foliage, especially in spring, wilts quickly, and some flower heads may droop because they cannot get enough water quickly enough.

Some water should be brought to the boil in a saucepan, and a piece cut off the ends of the stems using a slant-wise cut. The stems to be treated are bunched together with their ends level, and then wrapped loosely in a

Filling Hollow Stems

Some flowers, both uncommon and common, have hollow stems and require special treatment. They should not be placed directly in water; the stems should first be filled. Water can be poured into them, either from a small watering can or from a fine-lipped jug. When the stems are full, they can be plugged with a piece of plastic foam. The stems are then placed in water in the normal way and will continue to draw liquid up into their hollow centres.

Left: Soaking the stems of cut flowers and leaves in water—often referred to as 'giving them a good drink'—is the most important part of the conditioning process. They should be left in the water and in a cool spot for several hours before arranging.

Right: Young, tender foliage and wilting flower heads may need the 'boiling water treatment'. This helps them to take up water quickly. About 2 cm of the stem ends should be held in boiling water for 30 seconds, and then put into deep water. Flowers and leaves should be protected from steam by being wrapped loosely in a cloth or a polythene bag.

Leaves take up water through their surfaces as well as through their stems. Wilting leaves can be refreshed by allowing them to float in a bath of warm water.

cloth to protect the flowers and leaves from the steam. The stem ends—about 2 cm—are held in the boiling water for about 30 seconds. The stems must then be placed in deep water in the usual way. Rubber gloves should be used to protect the hands from steam.

Immersing the Leaves and Leafy Branches

Because leaves take up water through their surface area as well as through their stems, they can benefit from being wholly immersed in warm water for several hours. A large bowl or sink is ideal for this, or the bath can be used for long sprays and branches.

This treatment also helps to clean the leaves, but if they are very dirty —as evergreens sometimes are in mid-winter—they can be swished through water containing a little washing-up liquid. They should then be fully immersed in clean warm water.

Grey leaves are the one exception. They should not be wholly immersed as they usually have a velvety surface which can become waterlogged.

Special Tips

Apart from the more widely known methods of conditioning cut plants, there are many other ways of helping to prolong their life. Some of these sound drastic, but in most cases they are effective. Some flowers require individual treatment that would not be necessary with other varieties.

Additives to the water. Various remedies have been suggested in the past to help prolong the life of flowers in water, such as adding a copper coin, gin, sugar, starch, or aspirin to the water. Recent scientific research indicates that a mild aspirin solution does reduce plant transpiration, thus prolonging the plant's life. Experiments suggest that half a soluble aspirin added to a pint of water could prolong the vase-life of cut flowers by as much as 20 per cent. There are now additives on sale that have been manufactured specifically for the purpose of prolonging the vase-life of flowers.

Above: Spraying plant material with water, using a fine misting spray, keeps the atmosphere moist. This prolongs the life of flowers and leaves by reducing transpiration.

Right: An inexpensive hairspray can be used to prevent grasses, bulrushes, and thistle-type flowers from 'fluffing' as they dry. The spraying should be done when they are first picked for drying.

Below: All leaves should be removed from lilac and orange blossom, otherwise the flower heads will soon wilt. Some of the leaves can be used separately in the arrangement.

A misting spray containing tepid water will help to keep a moist atmosphere around a flower arrangement. A small spray sold for use with house plants should be used, and the arrangement sprayed as often as is convenient.

Drooping flowers benefit from the Ikebana technique of re-cutting their stems under water to remove or prevent an airlock. The flowers can then be floated in water to revive them.

Hair spray helps to prevent bulrushes, artichoke flowers, and pampas grass from 'fluffing' – releasing huge amounts of small seeds—after they have been picked and have begun to dry out. The heads should be sprayed generously with the cheapest hair spray available.

Refrigerator storage can retard the life of flowers which are needed for a special occasion, and have had to be picked or bought before the event. Roses respond successfully to this treatment. The flowers should be conditioned in the normal way, and then stored in a polythene bag in the lowest part of the refrigerator until they are needed.

Pollen, especially on the anthers of lilies, can stain clothes badly, so it is often advisable to snip the anthers off with flower scissors. However, this does destroy some of the flower's beauty.

Mimosa keeps fluffy longer if it is kept moist. Store it in a polythene bag until it is to be arranged, and spray it with water frequently.

Tulips can be a problem to arrange because of their curving stems, and the tendency for their flower heads to turn towards the light. To straighten the stems, wrap a bunch of tulips tightly in damp newspaper while the stems are soaking.

Violets and Hydrangeas can take in water through their flower heads. They should be totally immersed in water for an hour before arranging.

Lilac and Syringa (Orange Blossom) need to have all their leaves removed so that their flower heads can get enough water. Separate sprays of leaves can then be arranged with the flower stems.

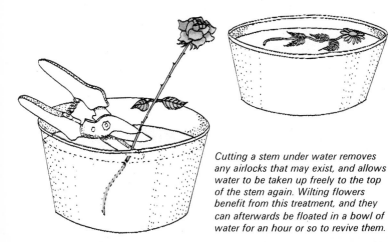

Cutting a stem under water removes any airlocks that may exist, and allows water to be taken up freely to the top of the stem again. Wilting flowers benefit from this treatment, and they can afterwards be floated in a bowl of water for an hour or so to revive them.

Plant Materials

Flower arrangements do not necessarily consist of flowers alone. Flower arrangers make use of a wide variety of plant materials in their arrangements. The following are frequently used, either alone or together, to create decorative arrangements: flowers, tree blossoms, leaves, ferns, grasses, moss, berries, fruit, nuts, vegetables, cones, seedheads, catkins, driftwood, tree bark, bare branches, stems, and fungi. Within each of these categories there is an enormous variety of size, shape, colour, and texture. And they may be used fresh, dried, preserved, dyed, or varnished. Leaves can be 'skeletonized', and stems twisted into interesting shapes. Apart from living plant material, an arrangement may also include stones, pebbles, shells, feathers, fabrics, ornaments, or candles, giving an infinite variety of combinations.

Plant materials can be divided roughly into three different shape categories. There are the fine and pointed shapes, the round or triangular shapes, and the in-between shapes and the bushy shapes.

FINE POINTED SHAPES

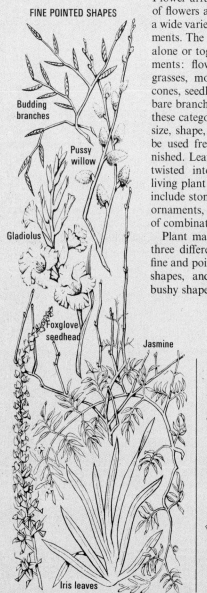

Budding branches

Pussy willow

Gladiolus

Foxglove seedhead

Jasmine

Iris leaves

ROUND OR TRIANGULAR SHAPES

Ivy

Tulips

Apples

Using the Shapes
Most successful flower arrangements will use a combination of the three basic shapes of plant materials. Traditional massed arrangements will use a variety of plants from each group, whereas a modern free-style arrangement may use only one example from each group.

The exception is the arrangement made from only one type of flower or plant material. To make a pleasing unity, this form of arrangement relies on the impact of colour and texture and the repetition of shape.

IN-BETWEEN AND BUSHY SHAPES

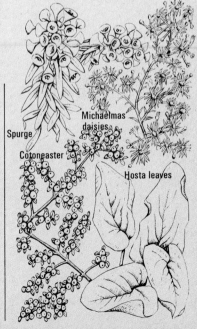

Spurge

Michaelmas daisies

Cotoneaster

Hosta leaves

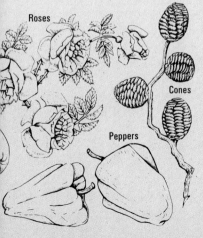

Roses

Cones

Peppers

Left: Colourful summer flowers massed together show a variety of plant shapes, sizes, textures, and colours. Variety is important to give contrast.

Below: The creamy-white daffodils and variegated kale leaves have bold shapes that contrast well with the curving stems of clematis buds, white blossom, and tiny forget-me-not flowers. Because the colouring is delicate, contrast in shape and texture is important.

Balancing Shapes in an Arrangement

In order to achieve a balanced design, the flower arranger should consider carefully the shapes of the individual pieces of plant material that are to be used. A traditional massed arrangement consisting of several types of flowers and other plant materials could be started with an outline of beech leaves and ivy. Ferns could then be used as 'fillers', and hosta leaves could, with effect, be placed low in the design. The round shape of a few roses and carnations would hold interest at the centre of the arrangement. The same approach can be applied to modern arrangements. Bare spikes can be set off with a few bell-shaped flowers, such as daffodils, to achieve a very striking effect.

Right: This design, with its strong vertical line, shows clearly the need for varying shapes and textures to give interest. Far less plant material is used here than in the other arrangements: only five flowers, three leaves, three gourds, bunches of seedheads, and tall plumes of grass.

33

Making an Arrangement

One of the simplest ways of arranging flowers is to stand them in a container that is taller than it is wide. This is also a useful and effective method of arranging flowers of the same kind. Garden roses or sweet peas can be arranged in a vase, primroses in a coffee cup, or spring blossom in a jug. The flowers should not be crushed together. Enough space should be left around them for them to be seen to their best advantage. The arrangement should not look lopsided, and there should be a pleasing relationship between the container and the flowers.

Using the Mechanics

If a more complicated arrangement is to be made, a suitable form of support is needed to keep the flower stems in position. A pinholder will be sufficient if not more than a dozen or so stems are to be used, especially if some are thick and woody. Fix the pinholder to the bottom of a dry container with three or four pieces of floral clay or Plasticine.

Wire mesh may be needed in addition to the pinholder if there are a lot of stems. The area of the wire mesh ;should be about three times that of the top of the container. The selvedges of the wire mesh should be cut off. The mesh is then crumpled up to fit over the pinholder in the vase. Several layers of holes should be made by this crumpling process, and the mesh should be shaped into a dome shape at the top—well above the rim of the container. Secure the mesh by crossing two rubber bands over it and the container. Alternatively, the mesh and container can be tied with string or reel wire in the same way as a parcel is made. If the ties show when the arrangement is complete, they should be cut away and not untied.

A foam anchor and a piece of water-retaining foam can be used in place of the pinholder and wire mesh. The foam should be cut to fit the container with some space left round it for watering. The foam should stand 3 cm above the rim of the container. When the dry foam has been cut to size it is then soaked in a bowl or bucket of water—the hotter the water the quicker it will be absorbed by the foam. When the foam has taken up all the water it can hold, it will sink below the surface. This

The arrangement of red roses, above right, relies on the colour and the repetition of circular shapes to produce a pleasing group. The arrangement, left, is less harmonious. The freesias and anemones lack integration, and the container draws the eye away from the flowers.

will take between 5 and 20 minutes, depending on the make of foam.

A very large arrangement with thick heavy stems can be made more secure by tying some 20 mm mesh over the foam block before beginning the arrangement.

Making an Arrangement

Once the plant material has been selected, prepared, and conditioned, the arrangement can be started. When attempting an upright design, the tallest stem—flower, or leaf—should be put in first. This stem should be at least one and a half times the height of the container to give a good proportion. It could even be twice as tall if necessary.

Place this tall stem towards the back of the pinholder or foam. At

this early stage it is important that the stem be firmly anchored in a good upright position so that the final arrangement will not look lop-sided, or as though it is leaning forwards or backwards. When the main stem is in position, one or two stems of the same sort are added. These should be slightly shorter than the first stem. Three or four large leaves are then placed low down in the arrangement with at least one leaf over the rim of the container. Flowers can then be added, using the initial large stems and leaves as a framework. In general, buds and smaller shapes should be kept to the sides of the arrangement, and larger leaves and open flowers should be placed towards the centre and bottom.

Design in Flower Arranging

Many creative people, including architects, painters, and sculptors, use accepted design principles in the course of their work. These principles generally relate to the scale, shape, and proportion of the designed object —whether it be a painting, building, sculpture, or flower arrangement. As a designer, the flower arranger should try to produce a design which is harmonious and has unity.

Balance

An arrangement should not look lopsided—with too much material on one side or the other. Nor should it look top-heavy, or give the appearance of falling backwards or forwards. If the tallest stems lean forward, the whole arrangement will appear to do so.

Proportion and Scale

A bunch of violets arranged in a large urn would look ridiculous, as would large chrysanthemums in an egg cup. This lack of scale and proportion is easy to see. However, less obvious mistakes can also be made, such as using leaves that are too large in conjunction with small flowers. A large number of flowers crowded into a small vase will also look out of proportion.

Rhythm

Good design should have a rhythmic flow. The viewer's eye should be

Left: Mixed pinks and reds in summer—gladioli, poppies, sweet peas, asters, dahlias, and gently-nodding pale green heads of quaking grass.

Right top: A tall arrangement of daffodils placed against dark shiny tiles gives a dramatic effect.

Right centre: A rhythmic design achieved by the use of a Hogarth curve outline. Chrysanthemums are arranged with berries and broom.

Right bottom: Small Alpine flowers, including blue gentians, delicately arranged in a cut glass bowl.

encouraged to move round the arrangement easily. Rhythm in a flower arrangement is often created by the repetition of shapes, lines, or colours.

Contrast or Variation

Too much of one thing—shape, size, colour, or texture—can be monotonous, and there is a need for contrast or variation. A flower arranger often uses a variation in colour, rather than a completely contrasting colour. An arrangement in cream, yellow, and yellow-orange, is more subtle than yellow with purple and mauve.

Dominance or Emphasis

Dominance is provided by using brighter colours, rounder shapes, larger sizes, stronger lines, or shiny textured plant material. If an arrangement lacks some dominant quality, the viewer's eye will never come to a rest. But mistakes can occur when the wrong things are too dominant in the wrong places. The arrangement then loses its unity. This would occur, for example, if a very large white flower were placed right at the top of an arrangement, thus upsetting the balance and destroying the unity.

Harmony or Unity

Harmony occurs when an arrangement has been given correct proportion, balance, rhythm, and contrast, and includes a suitable dominant element. The arrangement should also suit the container.

The Arranger's Eye

These design principles should be used as a guide for arranging flowers. But experience, and discovering mistakes by trial and error, is more valuable than learning a set of rules.

Shapes and Outlines

Flower arrangers often refer to the 'basic shapes' of their arrangements. Flower arrangement students may be taught to work within the framework of a geometric outline. The most commonly used outlines are a triangle—either vertical, symmetrical, or asymmetrical; an oval; a crescent; and an S-shaped curve—also known as a Hogarth curve. These outlines are 'good servants, but bad masters'. They can be a very useful guide for beginners who need something specific to work towards. The basic outline shapes help the student or beginner, at an early stage in their training, to achieve a pleasing arrangement with good line, balance, and proportion. However, working to these outlines can be very inhibiting to creative arranging if they are followed blindly and rigidly. The result is often a static, rather unhappy-looking arrangement where the flowers and leaves have been tailored to fit within a certain shape.

Every massed arrangement, as opposed to modern free-style design, will most probably end up with a geometric outline anyway; but this result should come from following the lines suggested by the plant material and the container. Or, alternatively, from working within the space and shape that the arrangement will occupy.

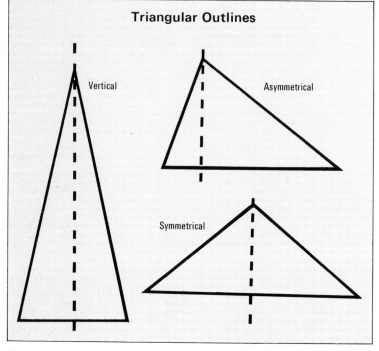

Triangular Outlines

Vertical

Asymmetrical

Symmetrical

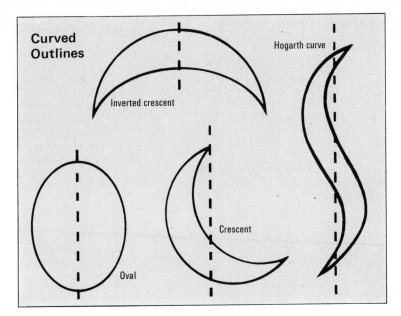

Curved Outlines

Inverted crescent

Hogarth curve

Oval

Crescent

A triangular shape will nearly always be pleasing to the eye. Its qualities are stability—the broad base—and movement or direction— the viewer's eye is drawn to the pointed top.

Symmetrical Outlines
Symmetrical outlines are fairly easy to achieve because the details on one half of the arrangement are merely repeated on the opposite side. Exact repetition is not necessary, and can make the arrangement look monotonous. A group of small flowers on one side can balance a large flower in a similar position on the opposite side. The focal area will be towards the bottom of the central line of the arrangement.

Asymmetrical Outlines
Asymmetrical outlines are harder to achieve because the point of balance —the same as the focal area—is not central. Larger, shorter-stemmed flowers and leaves will be needed to balance the longer, finer sprays and buds on the opposite side. Putting a pointed bud at the top left may balance a leaf at the bottom right of the arrangement.

Curved Outlines
Curved outlines obviously need curving plant material, such as shapely budding sprays—broom or pussy willow. With a crescent shape or a Hogarth curve, the point of balance —focal area—is again very important. As a guide, the top curving line should end above the focal point of the design.

These suggestions are to help, not to restrict, the flower arranger. There will always be times when the exception proves the rule. Experience and understanding of good design are more important than copying shape.

Colour

Colour is usually the most striking element of a flower arrangement. Most people respond to colour instinctively, and sometimes emotionally. They may remember 'the woman in the red dress' long after they have forgotten her name or her face. So, for the flower arranger, a simple working knowledge of the theory and vocabulary of colour is necessary. The flower arranger is concerned with the colours of paint.

The Colour Wheel
The colour spectrum is often shown as a diagrammatic colour wheel. This wheel shows the most important colours: the three primary colours—*red, yellow,* and *blue*—and the three secondary colours—*orange, green,* and *violet.*

A secondary colour can be made by mixing the primary colour on either side of it. Between the primary and secondary colours there are many other colours which shade imperceptibly from one to the next, making it impossible to say exactly where one colour ends and another starts. To simplify matters, the wheel shows only one of these intermediate colours in each case.

Tints, Shades, and Tones
Every pure colour can be modified by the addition of black or white. A *tint* is a colour with white added, making it lighter. For example pink

The Colour Wheel

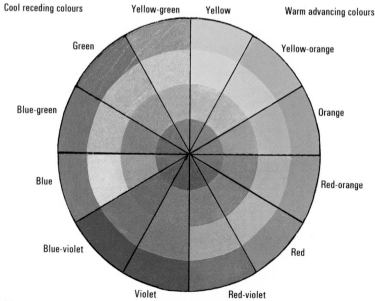

Cool receding colours   Yellow-green   Yellow   Warm advancing colours

Green

Yellow-orange

Blue-green

Orange

Blue

Red-orange

Blue-violet

Red

Violet   Red-violet

Tints and Shades

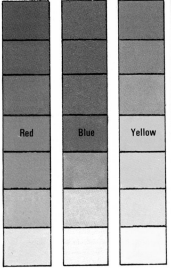

Red   Blue   Yellow

PRIMARY COLOURS

SECONDARY COLOURS

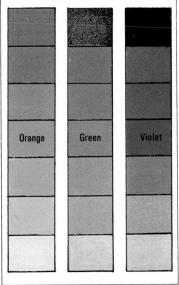

Orange   Green   Violet

is a tint of red, and cream is a tint of yellow. A *shade* is a colour with black added, making it darker. Thus, brown is a shade of orange, and navy is a shade of blue.

A *tone* is a colour with grey added. This makes a more subtle colour than the original. A tone can also be created by mixing one colour with the colour opposite it on the wheel.

Colour Schemes

There are two basic types of colour arrangements—*polychromatic* and *monochromatic*. With a *polychromatic* arrangement—'poly' meaning 'many', and 'croma' meaning 'colour'—many colours will obviously result. A *monochromatic* arrangement—'mono' meaning 'one'—will consist of flowers of a range of tints, tones, or shades of one basic colour. For example, red can range from the palest pink through to the deepest maroon: the whole range is described as monochromatic.

Analogous or *adjacent* colours lie next to each other on the colour wheel, and have one primary or secondary colour as 'parent' to the whole group. This is where toning colours are generally found. *Complementary*, or *contrasting* colours lie opposite each other on the wheel. With pure colours, the contrast is often harsh and brilliant as they show each other up to the greatest advantage. But the subtler contrasts of tints and shades can be very pleasing. For example, apricot with navy blue; pink with bottle green; dark brown with pale turquoise.

Neutral colours are black, white, and black and white mixed together making grey. They are sometimes called 'achromatic' and they do not appear on the colour wheel.

Warm and Cool, Advancing and Receding Colours

Colours are often described as 'warm or glowing', 'restful or cool'. Red, orange, and yellow are usually considered warm; blue, green, and violet are cool. If the colours in the wheel are viewed with half-closed eyes, the warm colours appear to be nearer, and the cool colours farther away.

As a result, the two groups are referred to as 'advancing' and 'receding' colours. The advancing or warm colours are more luminous—more visible in poor light—and the receding or cool colours are less visible.

The addition of white to any colour makes that colour more luminous. As a result, tints will always show up well.

Left: The analogous colour scheme of this spring arrangement is based on yellow. Tints range from off-white through cream and yellow to the yellow-orange of the tulips at the centre. Even the leaves are chosen from the yellow-green range.

Left: Although the flowers are all red, the green of the leaves is on the opposite side of the colour wheel: consequently this arrangement has a complementary colour scheme rather than a monochromatic one. If copper beech and other reddish leaves had been used, the effect would have been less brilliant and more subtle.

Right: The subtle colouring of this dainty arrangement is achieved by using mostly tints and tones and very little pure colour. The pinks warm up the cooler blues, mauves, and greens.

Arrangements in the Home

Most people like to have flowers in their home. Constance Spry, one of the best-known flower arrangers of this century, gave the following advice: 'Flowers in a room have a quality in common with the presence there of people, or of a fire, they bring it to life, make it look lived in . . . when once you begin to use flowers to adorn a room . . . you must think in terms of good line and balance, good colour blending and suitability of the whole to the background.'

Once the theory of colour is understood, it can be put into practice in the home with great effect. Anyone who has had to live with a badly thought-out colour scheme will know the necessity of choosing the right colours for paint and furnishings. There is an enormous range of colours available in most materials, so there is little excuse for anyone to be unaware of or unresponsive to colour.

The flower arranger has to make an assessment of the room in which the arrangement is to be placed. The arrangement should either tone in with the main colourings, or provide a definite contrast. An arrangement using warm, glowing colours will make a room seem bright and welcoming. The same arrangement, in the same room, but using different colours may have a completely different effect.

A picture or ornament can provide the inspiration for an arrangement using toning colours. The arrangement should either pick up some or all of the colours, or be made to enhance the picture or ornament by its shape, line, or style. In either case, the arrangement and its inspiration will complement each other.

It is usually better to have one well-thought-out arrangement or grouping of plant material in an average-sized room. Several small arrangements dotted around tend to get lost, and are less effective. Ideally the flowers and the room should be seen as a total picture. A good arrangement will brighten a gloomy room, and flowers can even be used to correct a room's dull or unsatisfactory features.

Style

The room and the flowers in it should complement each other in style. For example, an elaborate formal arrangement of pastel-coloured flowers and foliage would look out of place in a kitchen or a teenager's room, but would be very suitable in an elegant sitting room. Equally, a simple group

Right: The yellow flowers in this arrangement link with the gold-patterned wallpaper. The turned-wood pedestal complements the panelling and the clock.

Left below: Multi-coloured sweet peas arranged simply in a shell grace a polished writing table. Small, scented flowers of this sort are best used where their colour and perfume can be enjoyed at close quarters—as shown here or on a dressing table or bedside table.

Colour Schemes

Room Setting
Cream-yellow walls; golden brown carpet; orange and brown curtains.

To Make a Toning Arrangement
Yellow and bronze chrysanthemums; autumn-tinted leaves and berries.

Effect
Harmonious, pleasing.

To Make a Contrasting Arrangement
Blue and mauve delphiniums; green hosta leaves; green-blue hydrangeas.

Effect
Stimulating, possibly garish if overdone.

Room Setting
Beige walls; off-white curtains; grey and beige mottled carpet.

To Make a Toning Arrangement
Leaves preserved with glycerine, giving tones of brown; dried seedheads; grey leaves; white flowers.

Effect
Understated, could be monotonous.

To Make a Contrasting Arrangement
Bright red gladioli; shocking pink dahlias; deep red roses; a little foliage.

Effect
Warming, exciting.

Right: Flowers are most effective when grouped with and related to furnishings. Here, a Dutch trompe l'oeil is complemented by flowers capturing the atmosphere of 17th-century flower pieces. The association with blue and white Delft-ware strengthens the Dutch atmosphere.

Left: Copper beech leaves with orange dahlias and champagne-coloured chrysanthemums stand on a brick fireplace. The warm colouring complements the subdued red of the brick.

Left centre: Bold shapes are effective in an arrangement seen against light from a window. Wild arum leaves and spathes are simply arranged with contrasting new bronze leaves of sycamore.

Left below: The large massed arrangement shows well-balanced use of colour within a triangular outline. The blue flowers on the right side have yellow-buff flowers mixed in to balance the warmer rust colours on the other side.

of bright orange marigolds might be out of place in the same sitting room, but seem right in the kitchen.

The container used for an arrangement to be placed in a Georgian-style room with striped wallpaper, mahogany furniture, and velvet curtains will obviously be very different from that used in a room with hessian-covered walls, pine furniture, and boldly-patterned curtains. An alabaster urn would suit the Georgian-style room, and a chunky pottery container would be ideal in the other room. The flower arrangements also need to be different. The urn would lend itself to a massed arrangement of a variety of flowers and leaves. The chunky pottery container would more suitably hold a sparse design

of driftwood together with one or two brilliant dahlias.

Function

In the same way as different rooms are used for different purposes, the flower arrangements in them will also serve different functions. A small sweet-smelling posy on a bedside table is welcoming to a guest. However, the same arrangement would probably be quite lost in an entrance hall, where the welcoming flowers should be more emphatic. Bright, exciting arrangements stimulate conversation.

Space

In every room there are certain places where flowers look their best—on a sideboard or chest; on a bookshelf or an occasional table. In each case, there will be space around the arrangement. The size and shape of this space is important because the size and shape of the arrangement should complement it. A tall, narrow space calls for a tall, narrow arrangement, but a wide area needs a horizontal arrangement.

Windows

Flowers arranged on a window sill are often difficult to see against the light. In some cases, the light can enhance the lacey pattern of such plants as wild cow parsley or grasses; but it is usually better, in light surroundings, to have a backing of fairly solid leaves to outline the flowers.

47

Arrangements for the Table

A beautiful flower arrangement on the table can do much to turn an everyday meal into a special occasion; or provide a talking point for the family or guests. The arrangement should be suited to the occasion, and the table linen and china should be taken into consideration when planning it.

The meal may be a simple lunch for two, or a celebration party for many people. It may be a sit-down dinner, or a buffet with guests serving themselves. Any of these events may be formal or informal, and may take place in sunlight or candlelight. All these points should be considered when planning an arrangement for the table.

When the guests are sitting down, they will want to be able to talk easily across the table. Any flower arrangement that is more than 25 cm high will make conversation extremely difficult. Other considerations are also important. All plant material should be scrupulously clean as it will be near food, and seen at close-quarters. Strongly-smelling flowers or leaves can conflict with, and upset, the taste of food. It should also be remembered that flowers on the table are visible from all angles. The size of the arrangement will depend on the size of the table, the number of people to be seated, and the space needed for dishes.

Arrangements for a buffet table can be larger and much taller than those made for a lunch or dinner party. Raised containers, such as an urn on a plinth or a candelabra, are all suitable as guests will be standing and the arrangements will not be in their way. Because the guests may be moving about, the arrangements must be secure and not top-heavy, or they may easily be knocked over.

Right: A soft grey-green tablecloth and mauve napkins provide a foil for this arrangement: yellow and creamy-white spray chrysanthemums in a vase and fruit grouped with bay leaves on a separate plate. The rich purple-black grapes justify the choice of mauve for the napkins. Alternatively, the napkins could have been bright yellow to match the candles.

Left below: Tableware with a herb design is complemented by a red and purple-toned arrangement of flowers and fruit. Aubergines, blackcurrants, pansies, and small roses predominate in this design; the mauve colour is picked up in the napkins.

Complementing the Linen and China

Table decorations are even more effective if they are designed to link with the linen or china being used. If the china has a flower or leaf decoration, it may be possible to use the same flowers and leaves to create the arrangement. If this is not possible, then the colouring in the china could be matched with the flowers and leaves. If white or neutral coloured china is used, the inspiration may come from the table cloth, place-mats, or napkins.

Once again the style of the arrangement is important. A contemporary table setting using coarse linen place-mats, brown pottery ware, and paper napkins asks for a bold, modern arrangement with a few brightly coloured flowers or foliage. But a lace tablecloth, starched damask napkins, and bone china will suggest a more delicate arrangement with flowers such as roses, carnations, or pinks.

Special Occasions

Table flowers may be arranged in colours that emphasize the occasion. For example, white flowers are suitable for a wedding, or yellow for a golden wedding anniversary; pink, blue, or white for a christening. For a school, club, or regimental event, their own colours could be used for the arrangement. Flowers can also be arranged to highlight the type of food to be served: for example, an 'oriental' arrangement with a Chinese meal, or an arrangement of wild flowers to accompany a simple meal of bread and cheese.

49

Arrangements with Candles

Candles can give a specially festive air to an evening meal. They can either be used as part of an arrangement, or stand on their own. Several candles grouped with an arrangement of flowers or foliage on a single base make a good centre-piece for a table.

There is, however, one golden rule regarding the use of candles in this way: the plant material must be kept away from the candle flames because of the risk of fire. It is vital to remember that once a candle has been lit it will burn down! It must be extinguished before it gets near the flowers and foliage. This is particularly important when dried or plastic materials are being used.

If two or three candles are being used together in the same arrangement, it is better to have them varying slightly in length, with the centre one of three being the tallest. This prevents a hard, straight line at the top. The wicks should be straightened with a twist of finger and thumb when the decoration is finished.

Fixing Candles

If candles are to be used in separate candlesticks, they should be secured by placing a ring of Plasticine or Oasisfix in the base of the candle-holder. The candles will then stand firm and straight. To use candles as a part of an arrangement, they need to be prepared. Four cocktail sticks should be bound to the bottom of each candle, using adhesive tape. The ends of the sticks should protrude beyond the end of the candle by 4 cm. The sticks and candle can then be inserted into a water-retaining foam block, and the candle will be held firmly in place. And there is still plenty of room left for flowers and leaves.

If a pinholder is being used without a water-retaining foam block, four

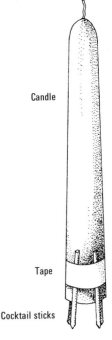

Candle

Tape

Cocktail sticks

Candle Holders

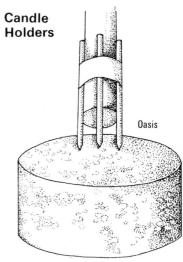

Oasis

Left: Making candles stand up in an arrangement can be a problem. One solution is to bind four cocktail sticks to the end of each candle with adhesive tape. The sticks are then pressed into a foam block until the candle just rests on top.

Right: A festive table decoration uses three slim red candles to accentuate the glow of traditional Christmas colours. The foliage that has been used includes ferns, rosemary, variegated ivy trails, and golden variegated holly. The green colouring contrasts with the red of the holly berries and carnations. White spray chrysanthemums and snowberries complete the arrangement.

cocktail sticks should be taped to the bottom of the candle, and the ends of these sticks cut off. Approximately 1 cm should be left, and the sticks will then wedge themselves firmly between the pins.

Party Accessories

At party times, a fantasy touch is acceptable, and other accessories as well as candles may be used. Feathers can combine well with plant materials, especially iridescent peacock feathers and ostrich feathers dyed in bright or subdued colours. Brown pheasant tail feathers look effective with the brown and beige colours of dried plant materials.

Ribbons can be looped, wired, and made into bows. They are then attached to a stalk, and can be used as a substitute for flowers when these are scarce or expensive. Coloured artificial birds can be given exotic tails made of grasses or leaves. Shells, fans, carnival streamers or masks, and wired sprays of beads can all be used to create fanciful arrangements.

Christmas Decorations

At Christmas time everyone makes an effort to have some kind of decoration in the home. The custom of using evergreens to decorate houses at Christmas goes back to ancient days. It seems that man has always felt the need for a mid-winter festival to cheer the long, dark days.

Traditional plant material for Christmas arrangements includes, holly, fir cones, mistletoe, and other evergreens. Useful evergreens are yew, ivy, laurel, spotted laurel, pine, and cypress. If any of these are available in the golden or variegated form this will help to relieve their somewhat sombre appearance.

There is also a wide range of artificial material available—artificial flowers, glitter, 'frost' and 'snow' in aerosol cans, and coloured baubles.

Preparation

Evergreen foliage can be picked in the second week in December. In cold spells the birds will probably attack the holly berries, so the holly should be picked as soon as possible!

Branches can be stored by laying them on the grass and covering them with a polythene sheet. This should be weighted down with stones. Alternatively, the branches can be placed in

Above: A Christmas bauble can be wired for use in an arrangement by placing a stub wire through the hanging loop and twisting the ends together. The loop and wire can then be covered with stem-binding tape.

Right: A decoration in traditional Christmas colours to suit a long oval or rectangular table. The red of the holly berries is augmented by the brilliant anemones. Golden cupressus gives contrasting shape and texture.

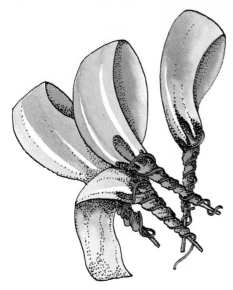

Left: Waterproof ribbon is not easy to tie. Separate loops should be made and the end of each bound with stub wire. The wire can then be inserted into Oasis, a garland, or the compost in a bowl containing plants.

Below: A fir cone can be wired by attaching a stub wire to the lower scales. The ends of the wire should be brought together and twisted to make a firm stem.

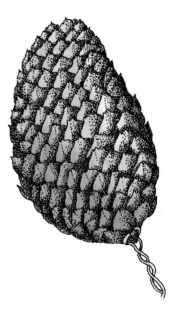

53

a bucket with a very little water in a cool, possibly damp, garage or shed.

Front Door Decorations

The tradition of placing a Christmas arrangement on the front door has long been used in America, and is becoming more popular in Europe. A door wreath or ring can be made on a wreath frame, which can be bought from a florist. Alternatively, a home-made frame can be made. To do so, a wire coat hanger should be pulled into a circular shape. Short pieces of evergreen are bound onto the hanger with reel wire or green garden twine. Cones, ribbons, artificial berries, and baubles can then be wired on. Waterproof florist's ribbon can also be used as it is colourfast, available in several widths, and not expensive. If a wreath shape seems too funereal, a solid round, oval, or elongated plaque can be made.

A large potato wrapped in kitchen foil, and wired to hang on a nail or hook, will provide support and moisture for evergreens. Holes are made in the potato with a skewer, and the evergreens inserted. Alternatively, a block of wet Oasis may be wrapped in thin polythene sheeting, and used in the same way.

The Entrance Hall

In a small hall, decorations may have to hang on the wall or be suspended from the ceiling. Dried or artificial plant material may be more suitable here. This will avoid water drips on the wall, carpet, or furniture. If there is room for an arrangement to stand on a table or chest, a winter landscape scene can be made using a wooden board for a base. A whitened branch,

A Christmas swag can be made from fresh pine sprays arranged with dried cones. The cones can be collected at almost any time of the year and allowed to dry out slowly. Dried leaves, sprayed gold or silver, can be used instead of the pine.

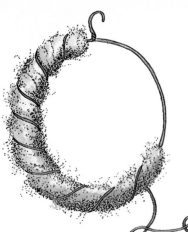

Left: A wire coat hanger makes a good framework for a hanging wreath. It should be pulled into a circular shape. Handfuls of moss are then bound onto it with reel wire or garden twine until it is well padded out. It is then soaked in water and allowed to drain thoroughly.

Making a Door Wreath

Right: Short lengths of evergreens, as well as berries, wired cones, and baubles, are attached to the padded ring. Ribbons are added as a final touch.

a few evergreens, cones and berries, and one or two imitation robins will give an effective seasonal arrangement.

A festive-looking yule log arrangement is an old favourite at Christmas time. The 'snow' is made by mixing a tablespoon of detergent powder with a very little water, and spreading it on the bark. Several holes can be drilled in the log to take two or three candles. Dried, preserved, or artificial plant material can then be attached by using pieces of Plasticine. Fresh flowers and leaves can also be used if a small container holding a piece of wet Oasis is taped onto the log, or concealed behind it. If the hall is rather dark and needs brightening up, preserved leaves and seedheads can be sprayed with metallic paint and sprinkled with glitter at once before the paint is allowed to dry.

Christmas Colours

Coloured lights are just as much a part of Christmas decorations as are arrangements of flowers, leaves, berries, and cones. The flower arranger must bear in mind that the Christmas lights will be in the same colours as the Christmas plant material. It is important that one should not be allowed to detract from the effect of the other. If red berries are placed under a red light they will appear to be white; green leaves in a red light look black.

Wedding Anniversaries

Golden—50 years Yellow flowers in a range of tints and tones from cream to apricot; yellow and lime-green foliage; oranges, apricots, peaches, and lemons.

Ruby—40 years A mixture of all the shades of cerise, red, orange-red, pink, and dark red foliage; copper beech; smoke bush; berberis; apples, beetroot, red peppers, and tomatoes.

Silver—25 years White flowers; silver, grey-green-white variegated leaves; a touch of pale pink or mauve to avoid a cold look.

Lace—13 years If it is the right time of year use cow parsley, a profusion of wild hemlock, gypsophila, and 'lace-cap' hydrangeas.

Wooden—5 years Driftwood; bark; branches; dried and preserved seedheads in tones of brown.

Fun Arrangement for a Children's Party

Special Occasions

Almost any occasion can be turned into a special event by the imaginative use of well chosen flower arrangements. Wedding anniversaries lend themselves to the colourful use of flowers, whether the party is a family meal or a large gathering.

Birthdays are an opportunity to give flowers that have already been arranged, rather than the usual cellophane-wrapped sheaf from the florist. This gift will be even more acceptable if the recipient is not a flower arranger. A basket makes a suitable container for a gift of this type. The most suitable shape of basket is shallow with a high handle —the arrangement can be made easily, and the handle will still show. A plastic dish or shallow tin is fixed inside the basket to hold a piece of Oasis. Mixed garden flowers can be used, or the simple varieties such as pinks, freesias, scabious, or chrysanthemums bought from the florist.

Hallowe'en calls for dramatic effects. An arrangement can be made using wood, red-hot pokers, brilliant red and orange dahlias, and apples. A witch, bat, or cat cut out of black

paper could be used as an accessory. A hollowed-out pumpkin, turnip, or swede with a candle inside makes a traditional lantern.

Guy Fawkes Night, also known as Bonfire Night, can be given much the same dramatic treatment by using any plant material that suggests fire, smoke, or fireworks. A 'guy' is easily made from two crossed twigs dressed in sacking, with an apple for a head, and features made with cloves or small stones.

Children's parties are another excuse for lively, imaginative arrangements. Children really appreciate

Left: A miniature landscape makes an interesting centrepiece on the table for a children's party. It is made of twigs, stones, moss and flowers arranged on a tray.

Above: A basket of flowers is a more attractive present than a paper-wrapped bunch. The basket should have a high handle, and foliage should be used to make a framework.

small scenes made on a base. The base can be a tray or plate. A garden scene can be made on the tray using moss, stones, twigs for trees, little flowers in scale, and possibly a few tiny toy figures. A 'moonscape' is topical and can be made from polystyrene ceiling tiles or packing. This is broken up and glued together to make a rocky landscape. Any strange-looking plant material can be added —chinese lanterns, poppies, or love-in-a-mist seedheads, teasles, and curly willow. Lollipops make good trees and chocolate drops and sweets can be added for fun.

Flowers in the Church

'Doing the church flowers' is a task that usually has to be shared by half a dozen or so members of a church congregation. Often, a person who is asked to help has little experience of flower arranging—but this lack of knowledge is generally matched by a desire to do the job well.

Getting to know how things are organized can often be as difficult as doing the actual flower arrangements. But most churches have someone who is in charge of the church flowers and will explain the 'ropes'.

Among the first things to find out are where and when the arrangements are to be done, where containers and flower arranging equipment are kept, and whether the mechanics are provided. It is also necessary to know where water can be obtained, and where to dispose of rubbish and old flowers and leaves. In some churches, the arrangers may be expected to supply the flowers; others will have a flower fund. The arranger may have to 'top up' the vases during the week, or this may be the task of some other volunteer. And, of course, it is important to find out whether the church is normally locked and, if so, where the key is to be found.

What to Take

It is usual for the arranger to provide foliage and to buy the flowers in the first place, even if later reimbursed. If any special kinds of flowers or colours are wanted they must be ordered in good time.

When setting out to do the flower arranging, a quick check that all essential items are available may save some exasperation later. These are:

Tools. Secateurs or scissors; cloth for mopping up spills: sheets of polythene or newspaper to work on, protect surfaces, and gather rubbish in; dust pan and brush.

Mechanics. Oasis; netting or pin-holders; wire; string or fixative for the mechanics: long-spouted water can; misting spray.

Plant Materials. Well-conditioned flowers and foliage chosen for their long-lasting qualities.

Buckets to stand cut plant material in, especially if there are several arrangements to do.

Above: Lime branches stripped of their leaves make a bold, elegant outline for an arrangement of large flowers.

Left and below: Large scale arrangements at floor level are usually created only for flower festivals.

Church Conditions

Arranging flowers in church presents different problems from arranging for home decoration. The greatest difference is in scale. Even in a small church, the spaces are much larger and the furnishings more massive than in the average home. If the windows are predominantly stained glass, the light may be poor in many corners and even at the altar. But large clear glass windows will make it difficult to arrange flowers on sills and ledges against the light. Because of the distance from which the flowers will be seen, shapes will need to be bolder, sizes larger, and colours more luminous. Altar hangings, cloths, and furnishings may be very ornate, and compete with the flowers.

Golden Rules

There are five golden rules about flower decorations in church. First, they should never be positioned in a way that obstructs the clergy or impedes church services and functions. Second, carvings, memorials, plaques, brasses and other features should never be obscured by the flowers. The purpose of the flowers is to complement them. Third, the wishes of the clergy should always be respected. Some churches do not have flowers on the altar; others prefer only white flowers there. Wedding flowers may sometimes be

permitted at the chancel steps even in Lent. In some churches, fonts are only decorated at the base and not round the top; and so on. The flower arranger should remember to consult first, arrange after. Fourth, if flowers are allowed on the altar, they should never dominate the cross and should, if possible, lead the eye towards it. Fifth, clearing up, especially near the altar, must be meticulous.

Altar Flowers

It is important to remember that the arrangements will be seen at a distance: consequently, flowers arranged simply will be the most effective. Too many different varieties of flowers and leaves will only give a fussy effect. Bold, clearly shaped flowers will show up best, such as open roses, lilies, dahlias, gladioli, chrysanthemums, tulips, and daffodils. These can all be easily distinguished, whereas sweet-peas, irises, larkspurs, and aquilegias are too confused in outline.

If the altar backing is elaborately carved, a mosaic, or a brocade or embroidered hanging, it may be necessary to use some 'solid' foliage to create a background against which the flowers can be seen. Laurel and magnolia foliage are useful for this purpose.

Colours are very important. The receding colours—blue, purple, and all the dark shades—can, from a distance, seem to be holes in the arrangement. The more luminous colours—white, cream, pink, yellow, and the palest tints—will, on the contrary, look bold and effective. When possible, the colour of the flowers should relate to the altar frontal in use at the time.

The flowers should, if possible, be

Right: This arrangement stood in a cathedral where the enormous scale of the building and the heavy, elaborate statuary could easily have dwarfed it into insignificance. The solution was to raise it up on a tall, wrought-iron pedestal.

Left top: The profusion of autumn flowers in this arrangement seems to be in danger of overwhelming the font on which it stands. But such arrangements have to be considered against the scale of the church.

Left bottom: Altar flowers must be large enough to be seen clearly from a distance. But they should not dwarf the Cross.

arranged *in situ*, after covering the altar cloth carefully. The arranger must see them in place, and walk back into the church from time to time to get a long view of the effect.

Altar vases with narrow necks make arranging difficult. But if the arrangements are not too large, they can be constructed in the hand, and then tied with string and inserted in the neck. A cylinder of Oasis can sometimes be placed in the top of the neck or in a matching candle cup fitted into it.

Usually, altar vases are in pairs, one vase standing on each side of the cross. The arrangements are not identical pairs but 'mirror images', so that larger flowers or longer sprays on the left of one vase will be on the right of the other. Before starting

work, the arranger should divide the flowers and foliage equally. According to the way stems curve and 'face', they should be used to right or left as they will look best.

For ease of working, vases should be three-quarters filled before any flowers are put in them. They can then be topped up when finished.

Pedestals

If flowers are to be arranged beside, but not on, the altar, this usually requires a pedestal arrangement so that the flowers can be seen well. Because pedestals are larger than altar vases, many new arrangers are daunted by the task. But it is not as difficult as it seems if some simple considerations are kept in mind.

The mechanics must be secure and

reliable to support the weight and the necessary length of stem. Cones are especially useful in spring to raise short-stemmed flowers such as hyacinths, daffodils, or tulips, so that the colour is taken well up into the arrangement. They will probably not be needed in summer or autumn.

Another consideration is that large arrangements need large flowers and leaves, not necessarily more of them. When large flowers are not available, several flowers of the same kind and colour can be grouped close together to get the same effect.

The general guidelines for arranging and making a good design do not alter in any way. The arranger is simply working on a larger scale, just as with a miniature a small scale is called for.

Windows

Flowers are often quite wasted in front of stained glass, and also distract the eye from the window. They are better concentrated elsewhere.

There are several ways of dealing with a clear glass window. The flowers can be arranged so that the outline is important and the detail and colour less so. A lacey effect can be achieved by using cow parsley, old man's beard, or budding branches; and a bold solid silhouette can be created with strong shapes such as iris leaves, fatsia, aspidistra, lilies, or delphiniums. Alternatively, a fairly solid background of dark leaves can provide a screen against which to arrange the flowers.

Weddings and Other Special Occasions

On special occasions, particularly at weddings, flowers are often allowed at the chancel steps. They are also often arranged in the porch, and on literature tables, choir stalls, and pew ends. The number of arrangements will depend on the size of the event and the money available: but unless it is a very big affair, they can usually be somewhat smaller and more intimate in these positions because they will be seen at closer quarters. Baskets are often thought appropriate, and should be arranged in a loose, informal style.

At a wedding, the bride should of course be consulted about colours. It is often effective to pick up the colours in the bridesmaids' dresses if the bride herself is wearing white.

Swag for a Pew End

This is a charming decoration even if only carried out for the first few pews. The method is to make a parcel of damp Oasis (about a quarter of a large block) wrapped in thin polythene. In order to protect the woodwork, it is backed with a thicker piece of polythene or one of the little trays used in supermarkets for packing meat. The whole parcel is tied up securely and suspended over the pew end with nylon fishing line or hooked wires. Then fairly short lengths of foliage and single leaves are inserted, and a few flowers added. The swag is decorated with ribbon streamers or a bow, using inexpensive florist's waterproof ribbon in white or in a colour that tones with the flowers.

Christenings

The font must be decorated in a way that does not impede the ceremony. Pink, blue, or white flowers are often chosen, but simple wayside flowers of all colours can look child-like and charming.

Right: A colourful arrangement of autumn flowers uses a small table as a pedestal; the container is concealed. The warm, advancing tones show up against the dark wooden screen.

Below: The strong pattern of the Norman arches calls for large, bold flowers. In such a setting, flowers should also have luminous colours, such as white, yellow, or pale pink.

Modern Arrangements

Contemporary styles, sometimes called *free-form, free-style,* or *free-line,* began to appear in Western countries in the 1950s. They have been much influenced by Ikebana (Japanese) styles and by recent trends in architecture, art, and sculpture. There are also other reasons why modern free-style arrangements have become popular. They use few flowers —sometimes only one or two—and this is an important consideration in an age when flowers are expensive. Also, flowers are not as readily available as they once were. Modern houses often have only small gardens, and many people have no gardens at all. Another consideration is that traditional arrangements may look out of place with modern furniture and decor. Bolder, uncluttered arrangements are more suitable.

Characteristics

Most arrangements in contemporary styles have certain characteristics in common. Very much less plant material is used than in traditional arrangements—possibly only a few stems with two or three flowers and perhaps leaves. Also, shapes and lines are bolder and simpler, and space is used as a positive element within the arrangement and around it whenever possible.

They also take more account of texture and colour; texture is given added importance, and colour schemes are often clashing and eye-catching. Containers are usually chosen for their bold, simple, geometric shapes.

Another characteristic of con-temporary styles is that artificial materials may be introduced if they have interesting form or texture. Such materials could include plastic tubing, steel, wrought iron, scrap metals, builders' materials, or poly-styrene packing.

Because contemporary arrange-ments are simplified, they are less naturalistic in appearance. Stems, for example, may be curved and looped, leaves may be cut to produce a bolder line, and flowers may be set at unusual angles.

Free-Style Designing

The technique of arranging has to be different from the traditional approach of creating an outline and then filling in. The aim is to be dramatic rather than pretty, and to achieve contrasts rather than gentle harmonies.

Plant material for modern designs is chosen for its bold shape and clean-cut lines, so that a rose or a dahlia is generally preferred to a Michaelmas daisy or aquilegia, a fatsia or aspi-distra leaf to cupressus or fern, curious seedheads to flowering spikes, and twisting bare stems or driftwood to gracefully curving sprays.

'Driftwood' is a flower arranging term used for any type of dried wood, root, or bark. Well-shaped,

Modern styles require a minimum of plant material to create an effect. Here, a twist of driftwood, two stems of lilies, and two of freesias have been arranged in a rectangular pottery container.

Above: This asymmetrical design uses less plant material than some traditional arrangements, but is not really modern in concept as space is not consciously used.

Left: The bare branches, bold orchids, and Scandinavian glass container are typical of modern arrangements.

Right: A design of dogwood stems and orchids shows Japanese influence.

unusual pieces are invaluable in modern designing. They may be used as a feature, or simply as a means of hiding mechanics.

It is sometimes difficult to make an awkwardly-shaped piece of driftwood stand well, but special clamps may be bought for this purpose. They hold the wood with a screw and can then be impaled on an ordinary pinholder. Alternatively, a piece of wood can be screwed to a base, and can then be cut and shaped to balance or have small pieces of wood glued on to act as legs. Freestanding pieces can be used decoratively on their own as examples of Nature's sculpture.

Mechanics should be no larger than is absolutely necessary. Because large pieces of foam are difficult to hide, a pinholder is usually better. Cover-ups for these mechanics can include stones and pebbles, broken windscreen glass, marbles, washed pieces of coal, and coffee beans.

Containers will be in simple geometric shapes with interesting textures. Modern hand-thrown pottery, building pipes or blocks, household discards, and 'found objects' may each prove suitable.

The Arrangement

Start by placing one piece of bold outline material in an interesting relationship with the container. Try several positions, not necessarily in the line of natural growth. Then consider the effect. Look at the spaces that have been created. If the arrangement appears unbalanced, it may be necessary to select another piece of plant material of quite different form to try to balance the design visually.

The next step is to add a second piece of material relating to the first —either the same type of plant material or something echoing its line, colour, or shape. The arrangement then has to be re-balanced with this addition. It may now have to be considered whether some form of dominance or emphasis is needed in order to knit the whole design together. A round shape might be tried in several places, then perhaps a second, and even a third if needed. Practice in this way with a variety of plant materials, both dried and preserved, helps in developing an eye for exciting balance and a feeling for the use of space.

Ikebana

A traditional Ikebana arrangement shows to good effect in a natural setting.

The Japanese style of flower arranging has long been recognized as an art form in eastern Asia. Known as *Ikebana*, it is often more restrained in its use of flowers and branches than the traditional massed styles of Western countries.

Ikebana originated in the 6th century AD when rules were formulated for the arrangement of temple flowers by priests. By the 13th century, styles had been simplified and had attained an austere beauty, and flower arrangement had become a leisure activity of the nobility. Until this century, the principal arrangers in Japan have been men. But today, Japanese boys and girls are taught flower arranging, and it is still revered as an art form.

Usually, the plant materials used in an arrangement must have a connexion with each other in nature—growing in the same habitat, blossoming at the same time, and so on.

Following the teaching of the Sogetsu School, one of the largest modern schools of Ikebana, each of the three main placements has a name and represents a specific idea. The longest stem, called *Shin*, represents Heaven. Generally, it consists of a carefully prepared, curving branch placed at a slight angle to the vertical. It is pruned to a length equal to the height plus the width of the container plus up to half as much more.

The next-longest stem, called *Soe*, represents Man. It is set at an angle of about 45° to the vertical, and is three-quarters the length of Shin. Again, it curves gracefully. The shortest stem, *Hikae*, represents Earth. It is placed at an angle of about 75° to the vertical, and like the other stems is curved. Usually, it curves upwards.

Jushis (helpers) are placed in position after the principal lines have been established; that is, when Shin, Soe, and Hikae are in position. Often they are flowers but, equally, they might be leaves. They are never placed regularly or symmetrically, and they reinforce the mood of the main stems, which has been set, largely, by Shin. It is important that a jushi should not be more than three-quarters the height of its main line.

The outline of a Japanese arrangement is usually clean and bold, though this does not exclude subtlety. In fact, the best arrangements are invariably both subtle and delicate. And they are in every case the products of thoughtful, careful, and accurate work.

There is much religious symbolism and philosophy in the way flowers are used in Japan, and for this reason Ikebana in all its implications is not easily understood in other parts of the world. But interest in the style is now widespread in Western countries, and Ikebana International has Chapters and study groups in many large towns and cities.

Above: In this arrangement, the twisted willow branches and the white lilies each have a symbolic significance.

Below: This simple arrangement uses a piece of driftwood as a container to hold auratum lilies.

Preserving Flowers

Just as a good cook needs a well chosen store of packet, tinned, or frozen items to supplement fresh food in the kitchen, so the flower arranger should have a stock of preserved plant materials to draw on when needed. It is both sensible and economical to have such a store, and for many arrangers building it up is one of the most interesting aspects of the craft. The long-lasting qualities of preserved materials contrasts with the short-lived beauty of fresh flowers and leaves.

Plant materials can be preserved almost indefinitely by various drying methods or by treatment with a glycerine solution. The Chart on pages 76 and 77 offers guidance on choosing a method.

The preserving techniques are simple, but success depends much on proper preparation. The materials should be picked on a dry day, and preferably after the morning dew has dried out. Only the best flowers, leaves, and seedheads should be used. Everything should be handled carefully, and prepared in the normal way. Snags on the stems should be removed, as should badly shaped leaves and florets. Over-crowded sprays should be thinned out by removing some of the leaves.

Above: Hydrangea flowers for drying should be cut when they are already slightly papery to the touch. The stems should be placed in about 2 cm of water, and the flowers allowed to dry out slowly.

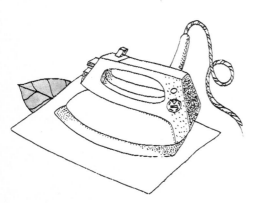

Left: Large flat leaves can be ironed under newspaper to speed up the drying process.

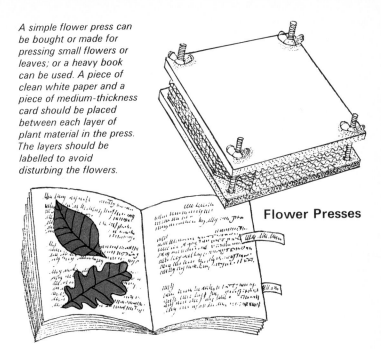

A simple flower press can be bought or made for pressing small flowers or leaves; or a heavy book can be used. A piece of clean white paper and a piece of medium-thickness card should be placed between each layer of plant material in the press. The layers should be labelled to avoid disturbing the flowers.

Flower Presses

There are three methods of drying: air drying, pressing, and the use of desiccants.

Air Drying

As a first step, all leaves are removed; if left they will shrivel. The stems are tied in bunches, with the flower heads at different levels so that they are not crushed. Then they are hung upside down in a dry, airy place. A garage is suitable in summer; in winter they can be hung in an airing cupboard or near a boiler. They should be left to dry until quite crisp to the touch.

Hydrangeas and heathers are usually better dried by standing the stems in about 2 cm of water in a jar or vase. They are then left, without adding more water, until they dry out.

Pressing

The simplest way of pressing flowers and leaves is to place them between the pages of a thick book, preferably one with non-glossy pages. The book can then be put under something heavy. Alternatively, a flower-press can be bought or made. Whichever is used, it is important to take great care in positioning the plant material so that it is not creased or its edges turned over. It is better not to overlap pieces. To speed up the pressing, some large leaves, such as chestnut, may be ironed between sheets of newspaper, using a warm iron.

As it is likely that pressed materials will be used for pictures, the longer they are left in the book or press, the more permanent the colour will be when they are brought out into the light again. At least six months is advisable. Stems are worth pressing, as well as flowers and leaves. They can be shaped into curves by sticking them down with adhesive tape.

Bracken, sprays of leaves, and ferns may be pressed between sheets of newspaper under a carpet. But they should be put in a place that is r ot walked over too frequently, or the leaves may move and become crumpled.

Using Desiccants
Thick, fleshy, or many-petalled flowers and grey leaves can be dried by using a desiccant. Desiccants are drying agents—substances that possess the quality of withdrawing and absorbing moisture from other materials. Those most often used to dry plant material are sand, borax, and silica gel, though it is also possible to use detergent powders. Desiccants should always be used in the driest possible conditions, because they also absorb moisture from the atmosphere. They can be used over and over again, provided that they are dried out in a very slow oven between each use.

Sand is the slowest acting of the desiccants, and is good on thicker petals. Silver sand is the best, but any other kind can be used so long as it is washed and dried out first.

Borax, a fine white powder obtainable from most chemists, is especially suitable for very delicate flowers. But it is inclined to cling to the dried petals and needs to be brushed away with a fine brush of the type used for watercolour painting.

Silica gel crystals are the most expensive, but when they are used most flowers take only two to four days to dry. If left longer, they become too brittle.

Before drying, the flower should be wired. The stem can be cut to within 2 cm of the flower head, and a hooked stub wire pushed gently through the centre of the flower to come out by the cut stem. The wire can then be coiled up so as to take up less room during drying.

Method. The method of use is the same whichever desiccant is used. A layer of desiccant is put into the bottom of a tin, cardboard box, or plastic container with a lid. Most of the stem is cut away from the flower to be dried, and a short piece of hooked stub wire inserted through the flower's centre to form a false stem. After the flower has been dried, this wire can either be replaced by a longer one or slipped into a hollow, dried stem ready for arranging.

The flower head is placed gently on the layer of desiccant. More desiccant is sifted over it, filling every crevice between the petals. This must be done slowly or the petals will crush. The process is continued until the flower is completely covered. Then the lid is put on, and the box labelled with the type of flower and the date.

When the flower should be ready (see the Chart), the desiccant is carefully poured off through cupped fingers, the flower being allowed to fall gently into the hand. The petals should be dry and papery. If they are not, the flower is replaced in the desiccant for a day or so more.

Any powder or crystal left on the preserved flower is brushed away with a soft paint brush. Petals that have fallen off can be fixed in place with a spot of glue applied with a cocktail stick.

not dry out. When this is done, a colour change takes place; all glycerined plant material turns brown, but the range of tints and shades is quite surprising. Box and choisya leaves become a pale biscuit colour; magnolia and beech are usually a rich tan; eucalyptus takes on mauvey-grey-brown shades; and broom and berberis may be virtually black. The final colour will depend on many factors, such as the age of the branch or leaf, weather conditions during the growing season, where the glycerine solution jar is standing, and even perhaps the quality of glycerine used. Anti-freeze liquid, as used in motor-car radiators, may be substituted for glycerine.

Generally speaking, this preserving method is most suitable for leaves. But there are some seedheads and a few flowers that will take up the solution, and it is always worth experimenting.

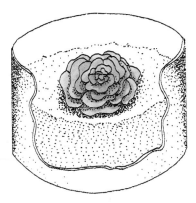

Above: The desiccant must suit the plant material to be dried. A 2-cm layer should be placed in the bottom of a container, and the flower placed on it and gradually buried. The petals must not be crushed. The container is then covered and labelled.

Preserving with Glycerine

As an alternative to drying, some plant materials may be treated with glycerine. Here, the idea of the preserving technique is not to take away the moisture but to replace it with a glycerine solution that will

When drying is complete, the desiccant is poured out through cupped fingers, and the flower allowed to fall gently into the hand. It should feel dry and papery: if not, the drying process should be continued.

The Glycerine Solution

It is sensible to use a glass jar so that the level of the solution can be seen at all times. A bottle of glycerine is emptied into the jar together with twice its volume of very hot water. After being stirred thoroughly, the solution may be used immediately.

The stems are prepared, and are then placed upright in 5 to 8 cm of solution. They are left there until the whole of each leaf has changed colour. This is easy to see, as the liquid first shows along the veins, then spreads over the whole of the leaf. It is possible to pack many stems into a jar, but some space must be left for air to circulate between the sprays. And the level of the liquid must not be allowed to drop so low that the stem ends dry out.

Some leaves, such as aspidistra and ivy, absorb the liquid very slowly, and the tips may dry out before the solution reaches them. These leaves can either be mopped from time to time with a swab of cotton wool dipped in the solution, or they can be wholly immersed in glycerine solution poured into a low dish.

Storage and Aftercare

Preserved materials must be stored in a dry place or mildew may develop. This may mean that they have to be kept in a cupboard in the house, because a garden shed or unheated garage is usually too damp in winter. Flowers and leaves should be packed loosely in cardboard boxes; long boxes can usually be had from a florist's shop for the asking. Poly-

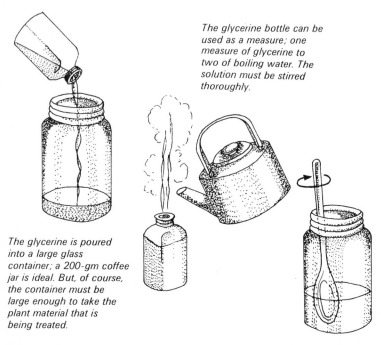

The glycerine bottle can be used as a measure; one measure of glycerine to two of boiling water. The solution must be stirred thoroughly.

The glycerine is poured into a large glass container; a 200-gm coffee jar is ideal. But, of course, the container must be large enough to take the plant material that is being treated.

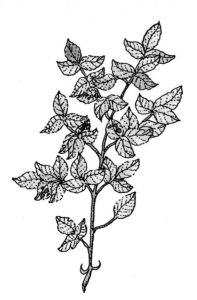

The plant material to be glycerined is prepared carefully. Marked or damaged leaves are removed, snags and thorns cut away or broken off, and overcrowded leaves thinned to improve the shape.

The prepared stems are placed in the glycerine solution. It is not necessary to wait until the liquid has cooled down. The jar should be kept topped-up to prevent the stems drying out during processing.

thene packing should not be used, as this conserves moisture and tends to cause 'sweating'.

Flowers dried in desiccant are very brittle and require special care. If a piece of dry Oasis is laid in the bottom of a deep box, wire stems can be stuck into it; the flowers stand upright and their heads will not be crushed.

Dried materials that have become mildewed are difficult to clean, but they can still be used silvered or gilded at Christmas time, provided that they are completely dried out again before painting. Crushed flowers and leaves should be refreshed and straightened before use. Stems can be induced to curve attractively by holding them in the steam of a boiling kettle and manipulating with gloved hands. This face-lift treatment is very effective for such flower heads as hydrangeas, and for flattened sprays of leaves.

Glycerined materials are more pliable and less likely to crush, but, if necessary, they can be revived in the same way. If dusty or dirty after long use, they should be swished through hot soapy water, rinsed, and thoroughly dried before being packed away.

Boxes should be labelled to show their contents. This will save much unnecessary sorting through fragile material, and damage to valued flowers.

75

Plants to Preserve

	AIR DRYING	PRESSING
SUITABLE FOR	Seedheads and 'everlasting' flowers	Flowers and leaves that are not fleshy or bulky. Small flowerheads useful for pictures. Leaf sprays
AVERAGE TIME TAKEN	2 to 4 weeks	4 weeks, but 6 months or more is better for pictures
COLOUR RETENTION	Better if carried out in the dark	Very good
FORM	Retained except that leaves shrivel	Flattened

Mature seedheads, such as:

Acanthus
Allium
Amaranthus
Artichoke
Bulrush
Globe thistle
Honesty
Iris
Lavender
Nicandra
Nigella
(Love-in-a-mist)

Pampas grass
Physalis
(Chinese lantern)
Poppy
Pussy willow
Teasel

'Everlasting' flowers
Acroclinium
Achillea
Anaphalis (Pearly everlasting)
Globe amaranth
Helichrysum (Strawflower)
Rhodanthe
Statice (Sea lavender)

Flowers:
Buttercup
Celandine
Cow parsley
Daisy
Freesia
Forget-me-not
Ferns
Grasses
Hellebores
Honeysuckle
Larkspur florets
Mimosa

Single petals
Daffodils (cut the trumpet in two)
Roses

Most leaves press successfully, but especially useful are:
Autumn-coloured leaves
Bramble
Bracken
Ferns
Grey leaves
Maple
Raspberry

Stems
Buttercup
Sweet pea tendrils
Clematis

USING A DESICCANT	USING GLYCERINE
Many-petalled or bulky flowers and grey leaves	Leaves, some seedheads, and a few flowers
1 to 4 days with silica gel or detergent. 2 weeks or more with sand and borax	2 to 3 weeks. Longer for some tough leaves
Excellent	Changes to a tint or shade of brown
Completely maintained	Completely maintained
Auricula Daffodil Dahlia Grey and silver leaves Hellebores Larkspur Narcissus Rose	*Single leaves or sprays:* Aspidistra Ivy Beech Laurel Box Laurustinus Broom Magnolia Camellia Mahonia Chestnut, sweet Oak Choisya Pittosporum Cotoneaster Rhododendron Fatsia Solomon's seal Ferns Whitebeam *Also:* Flowers of alchemilla, hydrangea, lime tree, sea holly. Seedheads of antirrhinum, dock, foxglove, iris, teasel. Catkins of garrya, pussy willow.

Flowers and seedheads can be hung up to dry in an airy place. They should be suspended head downwards. A garage is a suitable place in summer, but is probably too damp in winter. When dry, the flowers can be stored in labelled boxes. The flower heads should be hung at different levels so that they do not crush each other.

Using Preserved Flowers and Plants

When choosing plants to preserve, the flower arranger should try to have some from each of the three 'shapes': pointed, round or triangular, and bushy. This will give a variety of materials ready for arrangement.

Once dried or preserved, flowers and leaves can be arranged in the usual way, but without water. Because no water is needed, they have a versatility that fresh plant materials lack, and they have the added advantage that they can be used for pictures, plaques, swags, and collages.

Mechanics

Some flowers and seedheads may need to have a wire stem inserted. The wire can be bound with florist's tape in a neutral brown colour, or slid into a hollow stem to disguise it. Dry foam, which is similar to green water-retaining foam but usually brown or fawn in colour and more granular in texture, can be used to support stems. There are many different makes on the market. Dry foam will not absorb water and is therefore very light. When it is used as a support, the container will need to be weighted with lead, stones, or sand.

Dry and wired stems can also be arranged in Plasticine or floral clay pressed firmly into a container or onto a base. Stems can sometimes work loose, however, as the clay softens in warm conditions.

Fresh and Dried Arrangements

In winter, dried and preserved flowers and leaves combine well and economically; a few fresh flowers can be added for colour and emphasis. Chrysanthemums, in particular, look well with preserved materials. And as they are long-lasting when cut, an arrangement of this kind can last for two or three weeks before the flowers need removing or replacing.

If dried stems are arranged with fresh flowers and so have to stand in water or wet foam, it is worth while coating the bottom few centimetres of the dried stems with colourless nail lacquer or polyurethane varnish. If this is done, the water does not penetrate.

Pressed Flower Pictures
Pressed flower pictures should always be framed under glass. It is often a good idea to choose the frame first and design the picture to fit. Simple frames are best, and the glass should be non-reflecting.

The backing should be rigid. Hardboard, Daler board (used for oilpainting), and thick cardboard are all suitable. The backing is cut to shape, and painted or covered with fabric or paper as a base for the picture.

Method. The pressed plant material is laid out in a design on the backing. It should be handled as little as possible; tweezers or a flat knife should be used. Space is needed at the edges of the design for the frame.

When the design seems satisfactory, each piece is lifted carefully and stuck down with one or two spots of a latex glue applied with the tip of

Above: Pressed flowers and leaves can make charming pictures. Usually, the colours are soft and muted. The pictures should be hung away from direct sunlight to prevent fading.

Left: An antique frame can give a flower picture the look of a family heirloom. If the frame is not glazed —and the flowers and grasses have not been pressed—the picture will look three-dimensional.

79

a cocktail stick. The glass is placed carefully on top without causing petal and leaf edges to curl. The backing may have to be packed out so that the picture is firmly against the glass. Flower pictures should not be hung in direct sunlight or the colours may fade.

Pictures from dried, three-dimensional (rather than pressed) materials do not necessarily need to be behind glass. But if they are, a recessed frame is necessary. Such frames can be bought for the purpose, or sometimes it is enough to insert card or cording between glass and backing to give sufficient depth.

Greetings cards, calendars, and place mats can all be decorated with pressed plant materials, and make attractive gifts. The covering should

be of clear self-adhesive plastic of the type sold for covering books. Special card blanks are obtainable that include the protective covering sheet.

Plaques
The three-dimensional type of picture is often thought of as a plaque—a design fixed to a backing with some of the background left in view. It may be framed or unframed.

Method. A firm backing of hardboard or peg-board is needed, cut to shape and size. It is painted with matt paint or covered with a fabric appropriate in colour and texture to the flowers and leaves to be used. A piece of dry foam is secured in the centre of the plaque. Over it is a cap of wire mesh, hooked onto protruding nails that have been hammered into the

Right: A deep box or frame allows a three-dimensional picture to be glazed if desired. In this delicate little posy, pressed and dried flowers have been used. The flower heads have been glued down, and pressed stalks added separately to create the illusion of a gathered bunch.

Left: An arrangement of dried flowers, cones, seedheads, and leaves— preserved with glycerine— shows the wide range of brown tones to be found in preserved materials. Some are creamy white, some dark brown.

backing. This device will support a large and heavy design.

It is best to work with the plaque already suspended or propped up in a vertical position rather than laid on a table. When laid flat, the effect can be very misleading. Some pieces of plant material may be glued in place if this is convenient, but the use of foam helps to create depth.

Swags

For practical purposes a swag may be mounted on a firm backing. But the backing should be much smaller than the intended swag size, because it will not be part of the finished visual effect.

Collages

Collages are basically designs made from materials stuck onto a background or base. The word comes from the French *coller*, 'to stick'. Collages may be two-dimensional or three-dimensional and can use mixed materials—fabric, threads, shells, wood, seeds, and so on. A pressed flower picture is really a collage, but today the term is often used for an abstract design that is not a representational picture.

Collages offer enormous scope to the creative arranger to evolve new designs. They are free of the problem of mechanics generally met with in three-dimensional construction.

Fruit and Vegetables

Mixed fruits blend well with flowers on a dinner table.

Fruits and vegetables have decorative qualities that are often overlooked, but they are especially appropriate for table decoration. They have a very wide variety of shapes, colours, and textures. The economy factor is important, too, because they can be eaten after use as a decoration!

Obvious arrangements to consider are those contrasting the boldness of shiny red or green apples, tomatoes, and peppers with the soft bloom of grapes and plums or the velvety skins of peaches and apricots. Oranges and lemons provide unusual colour accents, and nuts give a range of brown tones and many textures. Pineapples, with their topknot of green leaves, make an impressive focal point in any fruit arrangement, and the pink stems and crumpled lime-green leaves of forced rhubarb look very exotic. Rhubarb stalks must be well soaked before use.

For an informal buffet or wine and cheese party, the humbler vegetables can be featured. Onions have attrac-tive flaky skins; the shape and orange colour of carrots contrast well with many duller and rounder vegetables; mushrooms will last without shrivel-ling throughout a party; pea and bean pods offer another contrasting shape; and young turnips often have attractive green and mauve markings. Celery, with its fresh green colour, should be well soaked before using; otherwise none of these fruits and vegetables need to be arranged in water.

A few fruits will dry successfully in an airing cupboard or over a kitchen boiler. Ornamental gourds and pomegranates change very little in appearance when dried, but oranges and lemons turn brown. However they retain their sharp scent. Even dried, shrivelled apples can have attractive crumpled shapes, with metallic hints of purple and green.

Ways of Fixing

When making a display of fruit on a

board, tray, or low dish, the difficulty is usually to stop the rounder fruits from rolling about. Cocktail sticks can be inserted into two or three fruits to join them together, or the sticks can be made to form little 'feet' by inserting three in the bottom of a round fruit. One or two 'pills' of putty-type adhesive may be enough to prevent rolling.

Bunches of grapes can be anchored with a stub wire twisted round the stem and a short piece of stick. The stick can then be inserted into a foam block or over the side of a container. Plastic grapes are very natural looking and could be used as a substitute when the real things are expensive.

Ways of Using
Fruit and vegetables piled in a random manner on a flat base are effective alone or with a few evergreen leaves —such as ivy, bay, or laurel—tucked in. A pyramid of just one variety of fruit on a raised dish similar to an old-fashioned cake-stand looks very attractive with a base frill of ivy leaves. And fruit can take the place of flowers in an arrangement if impaled on long wooden skewers or sticks. It will be top-heavy, so quite stout sticks are needed.

It is worth remembering that fruit looks rich and sumptuous if arranged underneath flowers and foliage in a tall or raised container. There should, however, be a colour link between the flowers, foliage, and fruits.

A larger arrangement of fruit and flowers is suitable for a buffet table.

Foliage

It is never easy to make an attractive arrangement using only flowers and no leaves. But this rule does not apply the other way round: an arrangement that uses only leaves can be very effective.

Leaves have a number of qualities that bring interest and variety to arrangements. They are worth thinking about carefully.

Shape

The most obvious difference between leaves of various kinds are their shapes, and the way they are grouped on their stems. A good foliage arrangement makes use of contrasting long, blade-shaped leaves with round and oval ones; clusters with curving sprays; ferns with simple shapes, and so on.

Size

Leaves range in size from the tiny fingers of heathers to the huge spreading fans of the giant hogweed, with every possible variation in between. Extremes of size can seldom be used together in one arrangement, but some variation is necessary.

Colour

Although it is usual to think of leaves as being just 'green', any garden or landscape viewed with a seeing eye will reveal many tones. They range from the darkest green, which is nearly black, to the palest lime green, which is almost yellow or white. There are many variegated leaves with attractive markings of yellow, grey, or white on green. And there are other colours as well—including the deep red of copper beech and the red berberis; the sometimes pure yellow of golden privet or holly; the blue-grey of eucalyptus; the woolly grey of lamb's ears; and the white underside of whitebeam. In addition, the arranger can use the brown tints or shades of glycerined leaves, from the pale fawn of box to the near black of broom.

Texture

It is easy for the arranger to forget the texture of leaves, though in a finished arrangement differences of texture can be appreciated from quite some distance away. For example, glossy leaves, such as laurel or magnolia, provide interesting contrasts to the matt surface of alchemilla, the woolly surface of most grey leaves, or the rough look of pine and yew.

Right: Autumn leaves arranged in a brass container exude a glowing warmth that never seems possible at any other time of the year. Unfortunately, they do not last long; but they are well worth arranging, if only for the enjoyment they give for a day or two.

Left below: The varieties of tones, shapes, and textures to be found in leaves are exemplified in this arrangement. Sword-like iris leaves mingle with curled and frilled poppy leaves, white-edged hosta, ferns, and artichoke. Green arrangements look cool and fresh in summer; they will last well if sprayed regularly with water.

Line

The line of a leaf, and the way it is carried on a stem, will affect the line of an arrangement. A curving branch of broom will suggest an altogether different line from the stiff spike of gladiolus or iris. And the arching hosta will give rise to quite different ideas from those appropriate to the flat rhododendron leaf.

Advantages

Foliage arrangements have many advantages over flower arrangements. An obvious one is that most cut leaves last longer than cut flowers, especially in the dry atmosphere of central heating. Again, a foliage group can provide a long-lasting background for a few cut flowers, which can be replaced periodically.

Containers

Containers of almost any style and colour are suitable for use with foliage, except perhaps delicate glass and porcelain. If a white container is used, some leaves with white variegations should be included and some grey foliage, so that container and leaves are colour-linked. Red and brown leaves look well in copper and bronze, yellow in brass, and grey in silver or pewter.

Pot-et-Fleur

The 19th century passion in many countries for growing aspidistras, palms, ferns, and ivies indoors has been revived in the second half of the 20th century. But nowadays there are far more varieties of house-plants available. There is much interest in purely foliage plants, although potted plants with flowers, such as chrysanthemums, African violets, and poinsettias at Christmas time, are among the favourites.

The grouping of several plants in one container, with a few cut flowers added to provide more colour and interest, is a form of flower arrangement that has developed over the last 20 years or so. It has acquired the name *pot-et-fleur*. Pot-et-fleur is one way of having the best of both worlds because the plants provide a permanent background arrangement, and flowers can be added as they become available. Usually, three to seven flowers are enough.

Making a Pot-et-Fleur
All the necessary materials should be assembled before work begins. Some of them—including plants—may already be available; others may have to be obtained.

Container. A container large enough to take four or five plants is

chosen; it should be deep enough to contain their roots when de-potted. A modern pottery bowl or casserole, a large bulb bowl, a copper preserving pan, or a Victorian washbowl are all possible choices.

Plants. Four or five foliage plants with a variety of leaf shape and size are selected: for example, a well-staked climbing ivy or kangaroo vine, a sansevieria, a fern, a begonia rex, and a small leafed variegated ivy to trail downwards. It is advisable to choose plants that require similar growing conditions, and that have some colour link with each other and with the container.

Other materials needed are: potting compost—well soaked; gravel or broken crocks for drainage; a few pieces of charcoal, to keep the water sweet; and a small tin, jar, or plastic carton to hold a pinholder or piece of water retaining foam. If this container is painted dark brown, green, or black it will hardly be noticeable.

Method. A layer of crocks is placed in the bottom of the large container, and a few pieces of charcoal added. Then a layer of soaked compost is put in, and the plants are removed from their pots and arranged in the container to form a pleasing group. Space must be left for the flower holder.

The roots are covered with more compost, each plant being firmed-in carefully. At the same time, the flower holder is put in. The container is then filled up with compost to within about 2 cm of the top to allow for watering.

Finally the cut flowers are added. It is usually most effective to have them all of the same variety and colour. Carnations, chrysanthemums, daffodils, dahlias, roses, and tulips are all suitable; but it will probably be necessary to remove most of their leaves to avoid overcrowding the plants.

Temporary Arrangements

For a temporary arrangement, the plants may be left in their pots and covered with peat, sphagnum moss, or compost. A larger, deeper container will probably be necessary, and at least one taller plant to give balancing height.

Left: A simple pot-et-fleur using two plants: Begonia rex and Philodendron scandens. The flowers are gladioli.

Far left: A more sumptuous arrangement, using plants, flowers, fruit, and driftwood.

Artificial Flowers

Artificial flowers lack the life and vibrancy of real ones, but the rising cost of fresh flowers encourages arrangers to consider alternatives. The idea of making imitation flowers is ancient. They have been used for centuries to decorate dresses and hats, and flowers fashioned from precious metals have been used as jewellery. In the 18th century, Madame de Pompadour, the mistress of Louis XV of France, even had porcelain flowers sprinkled with perfume planted in her garden to relieve the bleakness of winter.

It was probably the glut of cheap plastic flowers in the 1960s, often given away with packets of detergent, that prejudiced people against the use of imitations in flower arrangements. But even these stiff, garish products can be made to look attractive by spraying them with gold or silver paint, and sprinkling them with glitter at Christmas time.

Silk flowers, mostly manufactured in Asia, combine happily with fresh flowers and leaves to make a sumptuous display. Some of them are extremely beautiful. Fun flowers in crêpe or tissue paper can easily be made at home, and are effective in modern settings and at parties. They do not pretend to look real, and rely for effect on their size and bright colours.

The artificial flowers in this candlestick arrangement are made of china, and are delicately modelled. Stout wire stems are necessary to support the heavy heads.

Flower Arranger's Garden

Every flower arranger who has a garden, or has room to keep plants indoors, will want to grow some varieties that can be used in making decorative arrangements. Plants with interesting leaves are an immediate choice, because it is seldom easy to buy cut foliage in variety. When flowers are scarce or expensive, leaves are an invaluable aid to making a few blooms go a long way in an arrangement. Plants will be chosen for their flowers, too, of course, particularly those that have a long period of blossoming.

The Garden

It is sensible to try to see plants actually growing before deciding to have them in the garden. Illustrations in catalogues do not always accurately represent the real thing. Fortunately, it is easy nowadays to see a great number of plants growing in garden centres.

A good basis of choice is to look for plants, and especially colours, that will be useful for arranging at home. For example, a person whose lounge is decorated in browns and oatmeal colours, would probably do better to choose flowers in the yellow and orange range rather than in pinks and blues.

Underplanting is a valuable way of making the maximum use of space and keeping down weeds. Spring bulbs can be planted beneath shrubs; they will have finished flowering before the shrubs are in leaf and so will have enough light. Ivies, variegated periwinkle, heathers, and the small grey-leaved Hebe all form excellent ground cover under shrubs and provide good foliage for arrangements.

Some plants really earn their keep and are useful at more than one season of the year. For example the old-fashioned Honesty has charming spires of mauve flowers in spring; useful leaves throughout the summer, often turning purple in autumn; attractive greenish purple young seed-heads, and finally the mature 'silver penny' seedheads that provide an unusual colour in dried winter arrangements.

Not every plant is quite so versatile, but hydrangea flowers are lovely to use when fresh; they dry to a papery crispness for winter decoration, and the leaves take on attractive reddish

tints in autumn. Foxgloves provide long-lasting pinky mauve flower spikes in early summer, and tall seedheads that preserve well with glycerine for winter use.

Another point to consider is the type of arrangement that is desired. Small rockery plants and alpine plants will be useful for tiny arrangements. But an arranger interested in modern designs will find bold plants, such as fatsia, artichoke, and acanthus, more useful.

Indoor Plants

For a person living in a flat or a house without a garden there are house-plants to provide some cutting foliage, though less generously than from a garden. The ivies are always useful, especially the green and white *Hedera canariensis* or *Hedera* 'Glacier', and the larger leaved fatshedera. Aspidistras require little care and

produce large, graceful long-lasting leaves. Begonia Rex leaves have the most attractive markings in reddish pink, silver, and green. And there are many attractive ferns. A good house-plant book, a florist's shop, or a garden centre will show the extremely wide range of house plants now available.

Above and left: These two colourful and intensively planted borders are more extensive than most people can command. But they show the advantage of close planting: weeding and staking are reduced to a minimum. Though these borders were obviously planned for their beauty as part of the garden, they are also a flower arranger's treasure house. The tall flowers at the back would be ideal for use in pedestal and church arrangements. And the smaller plants could be used in the house.

Flower Arranger's Top Ten Plants

From the flower arranger's point of view, some plants are much more useful and versatile than others. Here are ten plants that are invaluable. They are easy to grow on most soils and in most situations.

It is sensible to learn the Latin names of plants in common use. The Latin nomenclature is international and precise, whereas many popular names vary from place to place. Of course, the Latin name and the

Alchemilla

Bergenia cordifolia

popular name sometimes coincide (dahlia, gladiolus, chrysanthemum, and narcissus, for example), but many plants have several 'common' names, each known only to the people of a particular locality.

1. **Alchemilla** (can be up to 60 cm in height), also known as Lady's mantle, bears graceful feathery, lime-green flowers in early summer. It is perennial and seeds itself easily. The leaves are round and attractive.

2. **Bergenia** leaves (25 cm, plus flowering spike of 15–30 cm) are sometimes called Elephant's ears and are tough and leathery. They last throughout the year. *Bergenia cordifolia* is the one to grow for the best shaped leaf, and some varieties turn red in autumn. Pink flowers in early spring are a bonus.

3. **Cypress** (*Cupressus*) comes in many shapes, colours, and sizes from miniatures for the rockery to tall trees. Most garden centres stock a good range. The yellow varieties suggest sunshine on cold winter days, and the yellow-green feathery foliage lasts a long time when cut. It is a useful foil to darker evergreens such as holly and laurel.

4. **Holly** (*Ilex*) is fairly slow growing, but is well worth planting. The variegated varieties are invaluable at Christmas time and, indeed, throughout the winter. *Golden king* is a yellow and green variety with few prickles, and *silver queen* is green and white.

5. **Hosta** (15–40 cm), sometimes known as Funkia or the Plantain

Lily, is a plant that flower arrangers have done much to popularize. Hosta is grown mainly for its leaves, though the spikes of mauve or white flowers also arrange well. Some leaves are plain green, some grey-blue, some have yellow or lime markings, and some have white edges or centres.

6. **Ivy** (*Hedera*) is even more versatile than Hosta, providing long sprays for outlines in arrangements and, single attractively shaped leaves. Again there is a range of sizes and colours varying from dark to lime green, with yellow centres, yellow edges, white marbling, or grey and white marking. Ivies are not fussy about soil or situation, and will climb over a fence, shed, or old tree stump as well as along the ground.

7. **Laurustinus** (*Viburnum tinus*) is an evergreen shrub with attractive dark green leaves. It has pinky-white flower clusters for several months in the depth of winter.

8. **Mahonias** are hardy evergreen shrubs seldom much more than about 1 m high. *Mahonia aquifolium*, with leaves very like those of the rose, is long-lasting in water, and *Mahonia japonica* has bolder, larger leaves and sweet-smelling yellow flower clusters. All mahonia leaves take glycerine well and colour to a grey-brown or a rich tan.

9. **Golden privet** (*Ligustrum ovalifolium 'aureo-marginatum'*) is all too often seen as a clipped hedge, but makes a brilliant yellow specimen bush to cut from time and again. It is not quite evergreen, but the sturdy leaves often remain on the bush until the new buds cause them to fall off.

Ilex aquifolium

Hosta fortunei

Bushes grown in full sun are usually a brighter yellow.

10. **Senecio laxifolium** (sometimes also known as *Senecio greyii*) is 'evergrey' rather than evergreen, and will grow almost anywhere. It tends to straggle rather untidily, but will stand any amount of cutting. The yellow daisy flowers in summer are not very useful, but the buds grow in elegant sprays and are pure silver before they open. At any time of the year, there will be leaf sprays to cut, each leaf being grey-green on top and silvery-white beneath.

Flower Arranger's Calendar

Spring

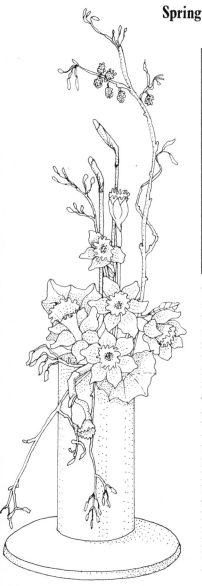

The container is two-thirds filled with sand, and the pinholder placed on top with a little crumpled wire netting secured over it. Then the container is positioned on the base in such a way that both form part of the design from the beginning. The tallest branch is made to stand at the back of the container, to left · or right as is appropriate, so that it curves inwards. It will need to be about twice the height of the container. The other branches are added, then the large leaves are placed near · the rim. Finally the daffodils are inserted, buds being placed to stand highest in the arrangement with open flowers lower down. The flowers are made to face in different directions. Two lemons can be put in a position at the base where their colour balances that of the flowers.

Things to Do

Seed packets should be bought early. Something new could be chosen to provide a seedhead for drying, different leaves, or an annual flower. Gaps in the garden should be noted and plans made to fill them with useful plants for cutting.

Several bases can be covered with fabric in tones that will have general use. Silver cake-boards can be used for round bases, or a handyman could cut rectangles, ovals, and tear-drop shapes from chipboard or ply-wood. Two strips of wood glued to the underside would make finger-holds.

What to Look Out For

Pussy willow showing silver buds.
Black ivy berries.
Forsythia, flowering currant, and curly willow to bring indoors to force into leaf or flower.
New bronze fronds of sycamore.
Violets and primroses—not to be picked unless in the garden.
Norway maple's lime-green flowers.

Daffodils and their leaves are arranged with cupressus sprays and stems of Cornus mas bearing lime-yellow flower clusters. Many kinds of plant material are available in spring, but the arranger should choose those that suggest the growth of new life in the garden and the approach of long awaited summer days.

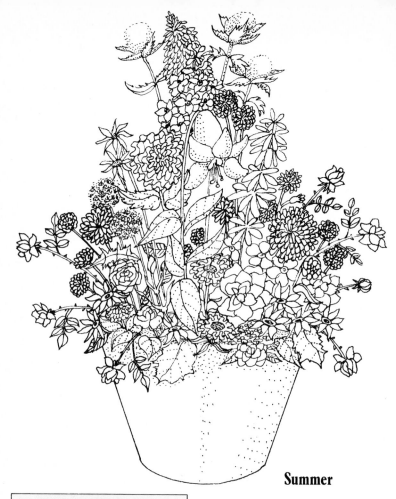

Summer

An Arrangement to Make

Container	A china vase or bowl.
Mechanics	Pinholder, with crumpled wire netting.
Plant material	Mixed summer flowers with round, bell, and spire shapes. A few dainty leaves —hosta, ivy.

The bright and glowing colours of summer: many summer arrangements show the profusion of the season's plant life.

There is no need for water-retaining foam, and the flowers will last longer if just arranged in water. The aim should be the loose, natural style often called 'the English style'. If colours are mixed, a very bright one can affect the balance. The most open flowers should be kept towards the centre.

Things to Do

Mature foliage can be selected for preserving in glycerine; also seed-heads as they develop.

A variety of small flowers and leaves can be pressed and dried for making into pictures in the winter.

Rose petals can be collected and dried for making pot-pourri.

Selected flowers and seedheads can be dried by hanging in bunches.

Bulrushes should be cut at the end of summer.

What to Look Out For

Blossom branches to bring indoors for forcing.

Uncurling fern and bracken fronds.

Lime trees in flower—the leaves being stripped to leave winged flowers and fruits. They can be used fresh or preserved with glycerine.

Orange berries of wild arum in ditches and hedgerows.

Cow parsley and wild hemlock by the roadside.

An Arrangement to Make

Container	Copper or earthenware jug or mug.
Mechanics	Pinholder, with crumpled wire netting; or wet or dry foam can be wedged into the neck of a container.
Plant material	*Fresh* Beech sprays turning colour, or copper beech. Sprays of berries. Mahonia leaves in autumn tints. Dahlias. Montbretia seedheads. *Preserved* Glycerined beech sprays. Teasels, ivy seedpods. Pressed bracken or ferns. Dried heads of yellow achillea, or hydrangeas. Cones, seedheads.

Autumn

At this time of year, preserved and dried materials do not look out of place as they sometimes do in summer. On the other hand, there is still quite a lot of fresh material to be used before early frosts take some of the flowers—dahlias, for example.

It is not necessary to choose between one and the other; fresh and dried can be mixed. Because autumn tones are warm or golden, a copper container sets them off well. The tallest stems should be placed on the handle side of the jug, and arranged with slightly asymmetrical balance.

Things to Do

Colourful autumn leaves can be pressed.

The harvesting of seedheads should be completed.

The last leaf sprays can be glycerined before they begin to turn colour.

Specially prepared bulbs should be planted for Christmas flowering.

Bracken can be pressed under the carpet.

Corn cobs and artichoke heads can be dried for winter use.

Seeds of all kinds can be collected.

Artificial flowers should be made for use during the winter, and, in particular, for Christmas.

Things to Look Out For

The bonus of blooms from a second flowering in a mild season.

A trough below a wall mirror holds a casual group of dahlias, Michaelmas daisies, acer leaves, and pink spindle berries.

Bracket fungi to dry out slowly in a warm place.

Old man's beard (mostly on chalky soils) to use and glycerine in its silky stage.

Orange berries in the bursting pods of the 'stinker iris'.

Beechnut cases to wire in sprays for 'flowers' in dried arrangements.

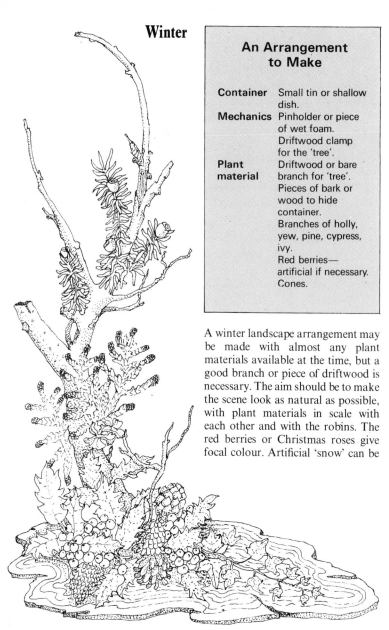

Winter

An Arrangement to Make

Container	Small tin or shallow dish.
Mechanics	Pinholder or piece of wet foam. Driftwood clamp for the 'tree'.
Plant material	Driftwood or bare branch for 'tree'. Pieces of bark or wood to hide container. Branches of holly, yew, pine, cypress, ivy. Red berries— artificial if necessary. Cones.

A winter landscape arrangement may be made with almost any plant materials available at the time, but a good branch or piece of driftwood is necessary. The aim should be to make the scene look as natural as possible, with plant materials in scale with each other and with the robins. The red berries or Christmas roses give focal colour. Artificial 'snow' can be

lightly sprayed if desired. As the container will not show, any ordinary tin is sufficient for holding water, but it is a good idea to paint it black or dark green so that it is not noticeable.

A winter group of red-berried holly, cupressus, and red carnations in a tall white vase brightens a dark corner of a room.

Things to Do

Flower pictures or calendars can be made up from summer pressings.

New containers can be looked for among household cast-offs.

Seed catalogues and nurserymen's lists should be sent for.

Planning should begin for next summer.

After Christmas, 'sticky buds' (horse chestnut) can be cut to force indoors.

What to Look Out For

Driftwood, bark and roots on winter walks.

Alder trees by water with last year's cones and budding catkins.

Rosebay willowherb spires.

Larch trees with long cone-studded branches.

Cones to collect and wire for arranging.

Inspiration for design from bare winter trees.

Entering a Flower Show

Some arrangers who have gained experience with flowers in their own homes will want to go farther and enter a local flower arrangement show or a horticultural show that has a flower arrangement section. It is always exciting to win a prize, but nobody should count on winning at the first attempt. There is always another show, and a great deal will have been learnt from watching other competitors, seeing the winning entries, and reading the judge's comments. Many exhibitors, even the most experienced, suffer from 'show nerves'. Some people just do not have the temperament to cope with this common affliction, but others find the atmosphere of preparing for a show stimulating and enjoyable.

The Schedule
The first thing to do is to obtain a schedule from the Show organizers: there may be restrictions on entry. Sometimes, certain classes are for members only or for particular cate-

gories of competitor. If there are any queries, there is always a Show secretary whose job it is to answer them.

The novice should choose a class that seems interesting, but preferably one for beginners where the competition will be less tough. One class is really enough for a first show; two at the most. The entry form and fee should be sent in in good time.

The schedule should be read, so that the conditions applicable to the chosen class are clearly understood. Staging and dismantling times will have to be noted, also the size of

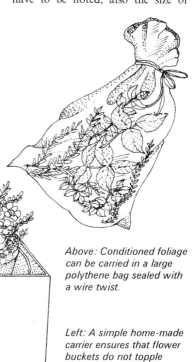

Above: Conditioned foliage can be carried in a large polythene bag sealed with a wire twist.

Left: A simple home-made carrier ensures that flower buckets do not topple over in a car.

the space or niche allowed, and whether judging is by any special rules or regulations. In the United Kingdom the majority of shows are judged under rules devised by the National Association of Flower Arrangement Societies (NAFAS). Copies of the rules are available.

Planning the Exhibit

If the chosen class has a title, it is quite a good idea to look up the words of the title in a dictionary. A dictionary definition can often trigger off ideas. If these ideas are allowed to simmer for a week or so—if there is time—they will probably take shape into a definite scheme worth trying out. One or two mock-ups are usually necessary, so plenty of time must be allowed before show day. It may help to make a rough cardboard niche the size of the space allotted, and to practice within this. Failing that, the space can be marked out on a wall in the kitchen or somewhere else. It is difficult to guess sizes: precision is imperative. At many shows it is all too evident that exhibitors have not troubled to check measurements when planning.

The container and mechanics are prepared first, care being taken to see that they will be absolutely secure. If necessary, flowers are ordered and collected no later than one whole day before staging time. This gives time to make changes if certain flowers are unobtainable. Foliage is cut and conditioned the day before the show and packed in a closed polythene bag. Then everything is put together in good time in a box or basket. Included are the containers and all mechanics, a base if needed, cutters, a cloth for mopping up spills, a sheet of plastic to work on, a watering can,

Many flower shows are held in marquees. They have an evocative smell that is entirely their own—that of damp cut grass and scented flowers.

and plant material. The schedule is taken, too, and the competitor's badge if one is issued.

Show Day

It is wise to arrive in good time, and find the allotted space early. After unpacking, experienced competitors start arranging quietly and in a deliberately composed way in order to calm any nerves. It is important not to move the tables or overflow into adjoining spaces: the respect of fellow exhibitors can easily be lost! When the arrangement is done, the temptation to fiddle should be resisted. It will be useful to walk away and view the arrangement from a distance, so that it can be appraised afresh. Any necessary adjustments can then be made, the water topped up, and everything made tidy; then it is up to the judge!

What the Judge Looks For

The first thing the judge looks for is that the exhibit complies in every way with the requirements of the schedule. If it does not then, unhappily, it has to be disqualified. Of necessity, competitions need to have rules, and these must be adhered to or it is unfair to the rest of the competitors. If the class has a title, the judge will consider how well the exhibit portrays and interprets that title.

Another broad requirement is that the whole exhibit be well-designed and in proportion to the space allowed. The arrangement and any accessories should relate to each other and form a balanced, attractive whole, using design principles well.

The plant material used must be interesting, appropriate, and in first-class condition. Every part of the exhibit should be well staged, neatly groomed, and properly finished. And, above all, the judge will be looking for some quality of originality or distinction that makes the exhibit stand out from the others in its class.

Knowing these requirements, a competitor would be foolish not to try to observe every one of them. A flair for designing and interpreting may be inborn and not easily cultivated; but the other demands can, with care and patience, be achieved by anyone. A little extra time taken in preparation may lift an exhibit into award standard.

Many new competitors do not realise that the judge assesses whether

Right: A summer flower arrangement show. Many of the niches on the background staging are semi-circular. The exhibits in the foreground have been entered as table decorations.

Below: Show exhibits should fill the available space pleasingly. The arrangements on the left and right would be disqualified. The centre arrangement would lose points for not making good use of the space allowed.

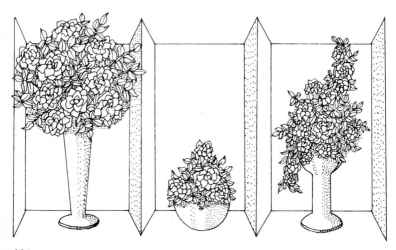

use has been made of the whole space allocated to each competitor, not just how good the actual flower arrangement is. Consequently, if an arrangement is too small for the space, it loses points however good it is judged solely on its own merits. If a container looks dusty or a base carelessly made, even more points are lost. The way parts are grouped within the space is important too, and the same design principles should be applied here as in the making of the arrangement itself. Even a title card is part of the exhibit and needs careful preparation. Most judges write comment cards for the exhibitors who do not win prizes. The unsuccessful competitor can learn from what is said—and hope for better luck next time!

Interpretative Arranging

In the early part of this century, some horticultural shows included one or two classes that asked for 'a bowl or vase of flowers arranged for effect'. The emphasis was to be on the decorative use of the flowers rather than on their horticultural excellence. This was, in fact, what is today called 'flower arrangement'. More classes for flower arrangement were gradually included, and in many contemporary shows the flower arrangement section is as large as all the rest of the exhibits together.

A later stage of development was for titles to be given to certain classes of flower arrangements, and competitors had then to make their exhibits not only decorative but also expressive. Today, most classes have titles and the interpretative type of arrangement is a feature of competitive work.

The soundest piece of advice that can be offered to the interpretative arranger is: 'The plant material should tell the story.' There is, unfortunately, a tendency in present-day show work to rely on accessories to do the work that the plant material itself should be doing.

Choice of Material

With a title such as 'Spring is Here' or 'Summer's Bounty' the choice of plant material is obviously limited to plants typical of the season mentioned. Chrysanthemums, for example, would not be a good choice for the first title.

Colour

Colour can play a vital part. Obviously, red, white, and blue are appropriate to patriotic titles in countries whose flags are in these colours, and yellow and white are suitable for an Easter theme. But colour has a subtler use, too. It can create mood and atmosphere: bright reds and pinks, for instance, suggest gaiety, and cool greys, mauves, and blues suggest sadness.

Form and Line

Form and line also play their part. Pointed leaves, sharp thorns, and jagged outlines can suggest strife, suffering, and anger; whereas smooth, flowing lines will represent rhythm and movement. Beautifully-shaped flowers, such as lilies, will portray serenity or sophistication.

Texture

Textures are often closely linked with form. Rough ones suggest masculinity, hard work, the simple life. Smooth ones suggest femininity, luxury, and leisure.

Association of Ideas

Association of ideas also aids interpretation. It is not difficult to see that wayside flowers and berries are appropriate for the theme 'Down a Country Lane', or seashore plants for 'Beachcomber'. But the first might also be used for 'Nostalgia' and the second for 'Heroes', to link with an exhibit interpreting 'Lifeboat Crews'.

A large exhibit depicting 'Royal Ascot'. It is formal and static, without perhaps fully interpreting the idea of a race meeting.

General Considerations

In any interpretative exhibit, every component part should help with the message. The container, base, background, accessory, and titling should all be chosen carefully to play their part. But it is very easy to overdo these items and hammer the idea home, rather than suggesting the title in a way that judge and viewers can appreciate with a little imagination. Selection is very important.

There is never one 'right' way to interpret a title or a theme. Every competitor will do so in a different way, and various aspects will be portrayed, to greater or lesser effect. This is what makes interpretative work endlessly interesting for the judge, the viewer, and the competitor.

An exhibit interpreting 'Fiesta' relies too heavily on the use of black lace to suggest a mantilla.

Advanced Flower Arranging

Even while the basic skills of flower arrangement are being learnt, there are various avenues open to the arranger who wants to learn more about the art.

Flower Clubs

Joining a flower club is an obvious first step. Few neighbourhoods are without one, and the addresses of local clubs can be obtained from the National Association of Flower Arrangement Societies, 21a Denbigh Street, London SW1V 2HF. Clubs can vary in membership from about 20 to 500, but most meet for a few

Judges at a show inspecting an entry in the flower arrangement class. They decided to award it second prize.

hours each month, some in the afternoons and some in the evenings.

Usually, there will be a demonstration by a visiting arranger or possibly a practice session. There will also be a sales table where flower arranging equipment and publications can be bought at reasonable prices. And there may be a plant stall, or library, or member's competition.

Many clubs hold competitive shows once or twice a year, often in association with their local horticultural society. Through the clubs, members hear about local flower arrangement classes and day schools, larger shows, specially organized days of interest, national events, visits to gardens, and so on. Sharing a common interest

with new friends is not the least of a flower club member's pleasures. A member may also have special skills in typing, accounting, catering, selling, or organizing to offer as a committee member.

Above: An entry in a local show depicts 'A Midsummer Night's Dream'.

Classes

Classes in flower arrangement are run by many local education authorities at leisure-learning day and evening classes. Sometimes there are day schools teaching flower arrangement, and flower clubs often organize short courses too. Longer courses, leading to a City & Guilds certificate, are held at technical colleges and colleges of further education. Part 1 of the City & Guilds course takes the equivalent of one day a week over a two-year period, and part 2 takes a further year. The syllabus covers the subject very thoroughly, and includes some botany and horticulture,

Below: A dramatic arrangement of gladioli captured the judges' attention and was awarded a gold medal.

as well as design and the other aspects of flower arranging.

Flower Shows

Experience at small club and horticultural shows is good training for entering larger shows—even perhaps the NAFAS National Festival, which is held annually in different parts of the country. The competition at such a show is keener and prizes less easy to win. But nobody should enter as a 'pot-hunter'—the real prize is what will be learnt in the process of competing. If a trophy is won, too, that is an exciting bonus.

Demonstrations

Through the flower club organization, a flower arranger can learn to become a demonstrator, attending meetings of flower clubs and other groups. A high standard of knowledge and proficiency as an arranger is first required. But for those with

A silver perpetual challenge trophy was won by this arrangement of King Protoa—the national flower of South Africa.

an extrovert temperament and entertaining personality, demonstrating can be very rewarding, though it is harder work than is often realized. The demonstrator's name is published to flower clubs after the passing of a test, and the approaches come from the clubs. A fee may be paid and, usually, the cost of flowers and travelling expenses are reimbursed.

Judging

Judging at flower shows is another interesting aspect of the art. It requires extensive knowledge of the subject, personal experience as an exhibitor and competitor, and the temperament to be analytical and to take reasoned decisions fairly quickly. Judges usually receive a small fee: travelling and overnight accommodation are paid for if it is a big show and judging starts early in the morning.

Teaching

Teaching flower arrangement at adult education centres is a part-time occupation. Preference is normally given to applicants who have taken the City & Guilds craft courses plus an extra year's (one day a week) training in teaching for the City & Guilds Further Education Teacher's certificate. Many flower arrangers also teach small groups of beginners at local meetings of clubs, the Women's Institute, the Townswomen's Guild, or the Girl Guides. Old Age Pensioners' associations and disabled groups in hospitals or day centres also value instruction in flower arranging. A few lessons are often included in homecraft courses for school leavers, and a local flower arranger is often approached for this.

Floristry

An amateur interest in flower arranging often leads to a desire to take up full-time work as a florist perhaps with a City & Guilds qualification in floristry. It is usually best to enquire from local florists' shops about the possibility of work to start with.

Voluntary Work

Offers to arrange flowers regularly at a church, local hospital, or old people's home are often welcomed. Flower arrangements give so much pleasure in such places. The local library, too, may like to have new flower arrangements made regularly.

Free-Lancing

Local hotels, offices, and shops often contract to have their flowers regularly arranged. It is quite hard work, so it is essential to be certain of what is expected before taking on such a job.

Arranging flowers at a bride's home, or for parties or other special functions, is a job many local florists do not have the staff to undertake. Arrangers often greatly enjoy an opportunity to take on such tasks because they offer a chance to work with more expensive flowers than can usually be afforded everyday at home. No fortunes will be made doing this kind of work, but the pleasure of the guests and the arrangers will be mutual.

Above: Judges discuss an entry before awarding it the 'Best in Show' prize.

Below: An arrangement entitled 'Portrait of a Gracious Lady'. It won first prize.

Flowers Have a Meaning

'There's rosemary; that's for remembrance . . . and there is pansies, that's for thoughts.'

Shakespeare

Flowers have been used as symbols for many centuries, and by people in all parts of the world. The gods and goddesses of ancient Greece and Rome each had a sacred flower or plant. The link between Venus, the goddess of love, and the red rose gives us what is probably the best known and most sentimental flower meaning of all. On St Valentine's Day, lovers still send and receive red roses.

The Greeks and Romans also used garlands of flowers and other plants as crowns to honour their heroes. Laurel stood for victors and victory; oak for bravery in battle. Winners in the famous games at Olympia were crowned with wild olive; at Nemaea with parsley; at Delphoi with laurel; and at Isthmia with pine. Bacchus, the wine god, was crowned with ivy

because ivy was thought to be an antidote for drunkenness.

Ancient herbalists believed in the *Doctrine of Signatures*, which stated that the curative properties of plants were indicated by their shapes and other attributes. The walnut, for example, convoluted like the brain, was reckoned to be good for head and brain disorders; and the yellow juice of celandine was said to cure jaundice. Popular flower names still in use today bear witness to these old beliefs—for example, Lungwort, Eyebright, Liverwort, and Feverfew.

But it was the people of the 19th century who, in their liking for sentimentality, brought the 'Language of Flowers' into everyday use. Scarcely a plant existed that did not have a message or meaning. Ladies kept albums with water-colour paintings of flowers, or with real pressed flowers, to provide a code-book for deciphering messages of love or messages of condolence in bereavement.

Poppy for sleep

Apple blossom for temptation

But not all flower messages were loving or sympathetic. A gift bunch of Fool's parsley, Foxglove, and a Japan rose could, it seems, have the meaning: 'You are silly and insincere and your beauty is your only attraction'.

Roses of all sorts generally stood for love or beauty, but a yellow one stood for jealousy or decrease of love.

The plant meanings best remembered today are:

Apple blossom	— temptation
Aspen	— lamentation
Bluebell	— constancy
Columbine	— folly
Crown Imperial	— majesty, power
Cypress	— mourning
Daisy	— innocence
Honesty	— honesty
Iris	— message
Palm	— victory
Poppy	— sleep
Primrose	— early youth
Weeping willow	— mourning

Today almost every country and state has a plant emblem. Some date far back into history, others are more recent. Examples are the maple leaf of Canada and the rose of England.

Crown Imperial for majesty and power

Rosemary for remembrance

Bluebell for constancy

Honesty for honesty

Copying an Old Master

As an arranger becomes more expert and experienced, much interest will be found in studying how flowers were used in past ages. And inspiration will be derived from flower paintings.

The colourful, exuberant flower pieces painted by the Dutch masters have a lesson for all present-day arrangers in the use of colour, rhythm, and form. Because these flower pieces were never actual arrangements, they are not easy to 'copy'; but it is a very good exercise to try to do so. The exact flowers may not be available, as they may be taken from several seasons—a result of artistic licence! However, similar shapes and colours can often be found in the garden, and it is amusing to try to use them as the painter did, sometimes showing sides and backs or revelling in the curve of a bendy stem and the touch of blue that is almost always present. The modern arranger may not wish to use all the symbolic accessories often crowded at the base. But the balance must then be considered if there are large flowers at the top. Fruit or a small, low, second arrangement may provide the balance needed.

Théodore Fantin-Latour, the French 19th-century painter, painted bowls and baskets of simply-grouped flowers. However, these seemingly artless arrangements were carefully thought out to achieve balance in colour and shape. They can be

successfully reproduced when the right kind of flowers are available.

The brilliantly executed wood-carvings of Grinling Gibbons (1648–1721) and his followers can be seen in a number of English stately homes and churches. They are a source of inspiration for swags and plaques of preserved plant materials. In the same way, garlands and wall drops that are the work of the designer and architect Robert Adam (1728–1792) can inspire an arranger to work in a similar style. Perhaps, in this case, the finished design should be gilded or sprayed with white paint.

Eighteenth-century tapestries, fabrics, and porcelain often include baskets of flowers which can be studied for ideas on how to use baskets today. Many books and photographs are available to show how the people of the 19th century arranged their flowers in tall trumpet vases and elaborate centre pieces.

When studying these past styles for details of the plant materials used, it is important to note the proportions between container and arrangement, and the colours. The settings and the overall effect of symmetry, elegance, or clutter are also worth studying.

Left: Théodore Fantin-Latour captured the beauty of fully-blown roses arranged informally in a basket. Throughout the ages, many artists have used arrangements of flowers as inspiration for their paintings.

Far left: Fantin-Latour's painting inspired this attractive arrangement. Mrs Sam McGredy roses have been placed in a basket, the lid of which has been propped open. An ovenware container hidden in the basket holds the water, and crumpled wire netting keeps the roses in place.

History of Flower Arranging

Flower arrangement is often thought of as a comparatively new interest, but its origins lie far back in Man's history. It is even known, from the quantity of pollen grains found in excavations, that Neanderthal man decked his graves with flowers more than 46,000 years ago. Paintings found in tombs in Egypt show how the people of the Nile valley used their flowers 2,000 years BC. The lotus flower, the blue water-lily of the Nile, was sacred to the goddess Isis. It was often worn in a headband and was also used to decorate offerings to the gods. Tall poles carried during funeral rites were adorned with the lotus, papyrus, and love-apples.

The ancient Greeks, and later the Romans, wore garlands of flowers on their heads on festive occasions. They scattered rose petals on tables, beds, and floors, and in the streets.

In Italy, at the time of the Renaissance, flowers were arranged in the churches, standing on the floor by the altars. They carried a symbolic message to church congregations who could not read: the white lily was the pure Madonna's flower; the blue iris also represented her as the Queen of Heaven; the orange lily symbolized Christ, the King of Heaven; and the columbine represented the gifts of the Holy Spirit. Violets were scattered on the floor to denote humility.

Men and women in England in Tudor times carried *tussie-mussies*, small bunches of scented flowers and herbs, as protection against the plague. Simply arranged bowls of garden flowers scented their rooms.

Dutch Painting

The beautiful, colourful Dutch flower paintings of the 17th and 18th centuries show magnificent groupings of flowers in urns and bowls. It is almost certain that these arrangements never actually existed. They were composed in paint from artist's notebook studies. Their exuberant mixtures of colours and graceful curving stems can be an inspiration for large massed arrangements today.

In this splendid 14th-century golden altarpiece by Simone Martini, the Angel Gabriel kneels before an elegant Madonna. Between them is a gilt vase holding Madonna lilies.

Ceramic Flower Holders

In 18th-century France, porcelain from the famous Sèvres factory included flower holders and bowls with perforated lids to support stems. In England the new Wedgwood range also included flower vases, and in both countries flower arrangements were in a simple, natural style, usually in pastel colours.

19th Century

During the 19th century, flower arranging was considered a suitable occupation for young ladies. In the grander houses, though, it was the duty of the head gardener and his staff to arrange the flowers. Elaborate designs in epergnes and trumpet-shaped vases graced the table at breakfast, luncheon, and dinner.

A wall fresco from Pompeii depicts three winged maidens gathering flowers in baskets. The flowers would have been used for making garlands.

Young ladies at balls often carried posies, and sometimes flowers were worn tucked into a 'bosom bottle' in the décollétage of a ball dress. Arrangements in this period used many ferns and grasses, and were usually packed with mixed flowers.

The Edwardians, on the other hand, rather favoured arrangements of one kind of flower only—the carnation, for example—with asparagus fern in cutglass vases. In the 1920s, there was a vogue for floating flower-heads in low black bowls, with a china bird such as a canary or a kingfisher standing in the middle.

The 1930s

It was not until the 1930s that flower arrangement really became a conscious art form. Constance Spry in Britain, made an immense impact with her graceful, subtly-coloured arrangements, not only of flowers, but of bare branches, seedheads, vegetables, and even fungi. She showed that any kind of plant material, both fresh and dried, could be used for decorative effect.

in a triangular shape. However, as flowers became more expensive and furnishings and decor became more uncluttered and sophisticated, many arrangers began to use fewer flowers and made arrangements that emphasized the line and textural qualities of all types of plant material. The use of space within an arrangement was seen as a positive function of design. The ancient Japanese art of Ikebana exerted a strong influence on this development.

In the 1970s a further step was taken towards abstract arranging—that is, arrangements that use plant materials purely for their design and evocative qualities and not in a natural way. The strongest influence here has been the work of such contemporary sculptors as Barbara Hepworth, Naum Gabo, and Alexander Calder, creator of the mobile.

One other aspect of present-day flower arrangement is unique to this century: the popularity of competitive flower shows where arrangements are judged, not only for the excellence of their design and use of plant materials, but also for their skill in interpreting the title of the class in which they are entered. This interpretative quality always generates great interest. Titles may range from the simple 'Breath of Spring' or 'Winter Wonderland' to the more complex 'Magic of Glyndebourne', 'Aspiration', or even 'Blast Off'.

It is hard to predict how the art will develop from this type of experimental 'do your own thing' arranging. Possibly the traditional massed styles will re-assert their dominance—if, indeed, they have ever lost it. What is certain is that an interest that has persisted for nearly 50,000 years is unlikely to die out.

Modern Arranging

In the 1950s there was an increase of popular interest in flower arranging. The boom in flower arrangement that began then still continues. There are flower arrangement clubs in Britain, Belgium, Germany, Monaco, Italy, Malta, the United States, South Africa, Canada, Australia, and New Zealand. In the United States alone there are no fewer than 14,000 garden clubs.

Throughout the 1950s and 1960s, the most popular style of arrangement in Western countries was the massed group of mixed flowers, leaves, berries, and seedheads, often

119

Books and Periodicals

Creative Flower Arrangement
Jean Taylor, published by Stanley Paul (General flower arranging).

Practical Flower Arranging
Jean Taylor, published by Hamlyn (General flower arranging).

Guidelines—Flower Arranging
Jean Taylor, published by Macdonald (General flower arranging).

The Complete Guide to Flower and Foliage Arrangement
Edited by Iris Webb, published by Webb & Bower (General flower arranging).

Design for Flower Arrangers
Dorothy Reister, published by Van Nostrand Reinhold (Modern flower arranging).

Flower Arrangement—Free Style
Edith Brack, published by Whitethorn Press (Modern flower arranging).

The Art of Flower Arranging
Marian Aaronson, published by Grower Books (Modern flower arranging).

Design with Plant Material
Marian Aaronson, published by Grower Books (Modern flower arranging).

Flowers in Church
Jean Taylor, published by Mowbray.

Collingbridge Book of Dried and Pressed Flowers
Jane Derbyshire and Renee Burgess, published by Hamlyn.

Pressed Flower Pictures
Pamela McDowall, published by Lutterworth.

Pressed Flower Collages
Pamela McDowall, published by Lutterworth.

Flowers for Pleasure
Kit Nichol, published by Lutterworth (Dried and preserved flowers).

A History of Flower Arrangement
Julia Berrall, published by Thames & Hudson.

The Rochford Book of House Plants
Rochford and Gorer, published by Faber.

Garden Foliage for Flower Arrangement
Sybil Emberton, published by Faber.

Shrub Gardening for Flower Arrangement
Sybil Emberton, published by Faber.

Wild Flowers of Britain
Roger Phillips, published by Ward Lock (hardback); Pan (paperback).

Trees in Britain, Europe and North America
Roger Phillips, published by Ward Lock (hardback); Pan (paperback).

The Flower Arranger
Published quarterly by NAFAS. Obtainable through flower clubs or by direct subscription from Taylor-Bloxham, Tyrell Street, Leicester LE35SB.

Flora
Published every two months by Stanley Gibbons Magazines, Drury House, Russell Street, London WC2B 5HD.

The Florist Trade Magazine
Published monthly by Lonsdale Publications Ltd., 120 Lower Ham Road, Kingston-upon-Thames, Surrey.

A painting from the great era of 'artists' flower arrangements': Flowers in a Glass Vase by the Dutch painter Jacob van Walscappelle (1644–1727). The arrangement probably never existed in reality.

Glossary

Abstract arrangement An arrangement in which the design is not limited by naturalistic ideas. The materials are looked at for their design possibilities.

Accessory Something used in an arrangement other than plant material, the base, or the container. Drapes and backgrounds are not classed as accessories, either.

Analogous colours The colours that lie next to each other on the colour wheel. They have one primary or secondary colour as 'parent' to the group.

Asymmetrical arrangement One in which the details on one side are not repeated on the other, though the arrangement, of course, still has to be balanced.

Background Mainly used in competitive work, a background is something placed behind an arrangement —for example, a piece of fabric—to set it off in some way.

Base Any object on which an arrangement stands. It must harmonize with the arrangement in size and every other way. Bases are not accessories.

Bloom An individual flower head.

Candlecup A cup-shaped device designed to fit into a candlestick. A support can be placed in it to hold an arrangement.

Collage A composition formed of plant materials and other components glued to a background.

Colour wheel A diagram showing the relationship between primary and other colours.

Complementary colours Colours lying opposite each other in the colour wheel. The complementary colour of red, for example, is green; red is a primary colour and green is composed of the other two primary colours blue and yellow.

Conditioning The preparation of plant material for use in flower arranging. Proper conditioning prolongs plant life.

Container The vase or other vessel in which the plant material is arranged.

Cool colours Blue, green, and violet are generally considered restful and cool. They are also called *receding colours*, because when the colours in the colour wheel are viewed with half-closed eyes, they appear to be farther away than the warm colours. *See* WARM COLOURS.

Desiccants Materials that have the property of abstracting moisture. Some of them are used for drying flowers and leaves.

Driftwood Pieces of weathered wood —branches, roots, or bark—sufficiently interesting to be of use in a flower arrangement.

Fixative Floral clay or Plasticine used to attach foam anchor or pinholder to the container.

Flower press A device used for pressing plant material when preparing it for making pictures.

Focal point The part of an arrangement to which the eye is immediately drawn because it is visually the centre of interest.

Fruit As the term is used in flower arrangement it does not refer only to edible fruits, and sometimes has a very wide application. Nuts, seedheads, catkins, bulrushes, fungi, and even grasses may at times come within the accepted definition.

Glycerine A solution of glycerine is used in one preserving technique. It replaces the moisture from plant material and does not dry out. Glycerined plant material turns brown.

Hue A pure colour at full strength.

Ikebana Japanese style of flower arranging. It is very restrained in its use of flowers and branches and the arrangements have philosophic implications.

Interpretative arrangement An arrangement that expresses a specific mood or idea.

Mass arrangement An arrangement of a large number of flowers with little space between blooms.

Mechanics Devices for holding plant material in place in an arrangement. *See* PINHOLDER; PLASTIC FOAM.

Mobile An arrangement designed to be suspended in the air.

Monochromatic arrangement An arrangement of flowers and foliage in tones, tints, and shades of one hue.

Oasis The name of a well-known brand of plastic foam, often used for any plastic foam. *See* PLASTIC FOAM.

Pinholder A mechanic consisting of a heavy metal base from which pins project. Stems can be pressed onto the pins as a means of support. Pinholders are also called *kenzans*.

Plaque A three-dimensional arrangement fixed to a backing with some of the backing left in view. It may be framed or unframed.

Plastic foam A light material sold in blocks and used for supporting stems, which are pushed into it. It can be easily cut to the shape required for any container.

Polychromatic arrangement An arrangement of flowers of different hues, shades, or tints.

Pot-et-fleur An arrangement of pot plants and cut flowers grouped in one container. The cut plant material can be changed when necessary.

Preserving Some plant materials can be treated in various ways to make them last for years.

Primary colours These are red, yellow, and blue; they are the 'basic hues'.

Scissors Flower scissors are short-bladed, and have a notch for cutting wire. The blades are often serrated.

Secondary colours These are orange, green, and violet. Each consists of a mixture of two of the primary colours—for example, green is a mixture of blue and yellow.

Shade A hue to which black has been added.

Swag Similar to a plaque but none of the backing is visible.

Symmetrical arrangement A symmetrical arrangement is one in which one side, broadly speaking, mirrors the other.

Tint A hue to which white has been added.

Tone A hue to which grey has been added.

Warm colours Red, orange, and yellow are generally considered to be the warm colours. They are also called *advancing colours* because they give the impression of being nearer than the cool colours. *See* COOL COLOURS.

The Publishers wish to thank the following for their kind help in supplying photographs for this book:

M. S. Alexander, Exeter: page 69 bottom. A.Z. Collection: pages 33 bottom, 35 bottom, 44, 59 bottom, 61 top, 79 bottom, 91, 92, 93, 112, 113. Jesse Davis: pages 32/33, 103. Paul Forrester/Arrangements by Jocelyn McCarthy: pages 40, 41 bottom, Cover. Sonia Halliday: pages 39, 56, 57 & 59 top, 61 bottom. Michael Holford: pages 8, 22. Japanese Embassy: page 68. Leslie Johns/Arrangements by Violet Stevenson: pages 30/31, 34, 41 top, 42, 43, 45 top, 46, 47, 50/51, 62 top, 65, 66 left, 67, 78, 79 top, 80 top and bottom, 80, 81, 82, 83, 84, 85, 86, 87, 89, 95, 97, 99, 101. Scott Lauder: page 69 top. Lancashire Life/Cyril Lindley: pages 108, 109, 110, 111. National Gallery: page 114. Scala: pages 117, 118. Harry Smith Collection: pages 9, 35 top left and right, 45 bottom, 62 centre and bottom, 66 right, 90, 105, 106, 107. Daphne Vagg: pages 17, 49, 115.

Picture Research: Penny J. Warn.

Index

125